Down Wind, Down River

for Jim & Cynthia

down wind,

New and Selected Poems

down river

William Witherup

WEST END PRESS

" We dared and say " p 15
Love, Whemp
Dec 5, 2000

William Witherup's poetry has previously been published in the following:

BOOKS
William Witherup, *Black Ash, Orange Fire: Collected Poems 1959–1985*.
(Point Reyes, California: Floating Island Publications, 1986).

Bill Witherup, *Men at Work*. (Boise, Idaho: Ahsahta Press, 1989).

Enrique Lihn, *This Endless Malice*. William Witherup and Serge Echeverria,
trans. (Northwood Narrows, N.H.: Lillabulero Press, 1969).

Antonio Machado, *I Go Dreaming Roads*. Carmen Scholis and William
Witherup, trans. (Monterey: Peters Gate Press, 1973).

Vicente Huidobro, *Arctic Poems*. William Witherup and Serge Echeverria,
trans. (Santa Fe: Desert Review Press, 1974).

Poems published since *Men at Work* were in the following anthology and
magazines:

ANTHOLOGY
Sirius Verse: Poetry For and About the Dogs in Your Life

MAGAZINES
*Guadalupe Review; The Kerf; Nuclear Texts and Contexts; Pemmican; San
Fernando Poetry Journal; White Heron Poetry Review;* and *wig*

First edition, October 2000.
ISBN: 0-931122-99-6

Book and cover design by Nancy Woodard

Distributed by University of New Mexico Press

West End Press • P.O. Box 27334 • Albuquerque, New Mexico 87125

This book is dedicated to three mentors:
James McGrath, James B. Hall and Sterling Bunnell

They know why and how they have mattered
in my life and creative growth

Contents

Introduction

Bill Witherup has lived nearly two-thirds of the twentieth century, from childhood during World War II to college in the Fifties to adulthood under the cloud of the Cold War, the Korean War and Vietnam. Born in 1935 in Kansas City, Missouri, he came west with his family as a boy when his father began seven-day shift work at Hanford Engineering Works, the atomic energy facility which operated under conditions of secrecy in eastern Washington during World War II. Mervyn Clyde Witherup held a job in this factory for more than thirty years, retiring early to allow younger workers to take his place—only to develop prostate cancer from radiation, which eventually led to his death in 1988.

As a sophomore at the University of Washington, the younger Witherup came under the influence of the poet Theodore Roethke; later, at the University of Oregon, he studied under James B. Hall. His vocation for poetry was estab–lished by the time he arrived in San Francisco, around 1960. Soon his poetry began to reflect local influences, including that of Kenneth Rexroth, master of the early years of the San Francisco Renaissance.

Emerging from the romantic concerns of his early poetry (American Indian mythology, the relations between story and landscape, the ruination of the planet by corporate greed) are his sharply realized love poems. A striking poem written in 1967 describes San Francisco as "a desert to the shyness of love." Although Witherup borrowed the image from the Chilean poet Enrique Lihn, the description of the woman that follows shows his own sensibility, putting human desire in close proximity to vulnerability and suffering.

In the late 1960s Witherup began to write from favorite places: Pacific Grove and Monterey, California, later adding Big Sur and Bixby Creek; and Aspen Ranch Road, outside of Santa Fe, New Mexico. Other poems are written in El Rito, the town where a lover lived in Northern New Mexico. Events and relationships are grounded in place; even "Thinking about Suicide" is located under "the far cold stars above Big Sur." Most of these poems show an assimilation of nature into the poet's practice, reflecting his deepening acquaintance with Zen Buddhism and his reading of the Chinese poets. As William Everson comments on his work of this period, "His technique at its best has been subsumed into his meditation until it unconsciously defines it. He has learned how to enter a poem, inhabit it, and then happily forego it."[1]

While in Big Sur, Witherup also wrote a major political work, "The Soledad Prison Poems," in 1970–71. Working as a teacher inside the prison following the Soledad Riots helped him to visualize guards in gas masks and yellow slickers firing their canisters of tear gas: "They are mutant locusts/laying eggs in the dead." In "Elegy for George Jackson," the martyr of Soledad, he confronts history by re-visioning Jackson's escape attempt: "I am cheering you toward that patch of light./This time you will make it." This poetry, like that of Walt Whitman and Pablo Neruda, engages the world, so that the political becomes personal.

The poems of the later 1970s and 1980s show Bill Witherup among friends in various places. Twice in the 1970s he taught as Artist-in-Residence in the public school system of Kentucky. Here he is at home not only with nature but with the people he meets, often reflecting the work they do. Back in California, his poems again orient to the work he does. They also show a close attachment to other creatures, including his dog, and draw wisdom from a comparison of the human and animal conditions.

> We love dogs
> because we have lost our bodies.
> Logos split us.
> No matter how often we copulate,
> we are destined to wander
> looking for our hands and faces.

Poems after 1983 reflect a darker time, in proximity to his dying father. Between Petaluma, California, where many of his work poems now come from, and Richland, Washington, his family home, he honors physical labor, toughness of mind in hard circumstances, and the memory of the atomic death. In one poem, he thinks of the carnage at Hiroshima and Nagasaki in stark juxtaposition to picking blackberries:

> Suddenly we go from blossom to berry to seed.
> Dear Christ, dear Buddha I offer
> One blackberry for each thousand A-bomb deaths.

His recent poems center in Seattle, a city of painful contradictions, which we recognize from the demonstrations against the World Trade Organization in the spring of 2000. Whether he offers us ribaldry, denunciation, or simply a record of his survival, his recent work reflects the spirit of the times: moral decay, the endangerment of the earth, denial in high places. Yet even the poetry of accusation can be touched by tenderness. Looking over the last fifty years, Witherup meditates on the eastern Washington of his childhood:

> Some will wander the scablands
> Near the abandoned Hanford reactors:
> Whistle for their feral dogs
> That have joined coyote packs;
> Apologize to the jackrabbits
> And the lovely, beating grouse.

The final poem of the book, "Envoi: Manic Depression in the Rear-View Mirror," is unreconstructed Witherup, still pursuing Beauty after his fashion, giving out all sorts of inadmissible confessions, defiant, obscene, and determined. The figure of Francois Villon, a favorite of Witherup's, comes to mind. In case you thought he was gone, he's not. He won't leave till he gets it right. Damn the Apocalypse; full steam ahead.

Added to this volume are translations from three major poets writing in Spanish. Antonio Machado, a poet of the "Generation of 1898" in Spain, provides us with a sense of the possibility of a poetry of place addressed to the human condition. Vicente Huidobro, the experimental Chilean poet of the World War I era, explores the possibilities of pure form enlisted as statement. Enrique Lihn (1929–1988), the introspective poet of Chile, applies his personal voice even to social and political subjects. These challenging tasks of translation help account for Witherup's striking combination of naturalness and intellectual penetration in his own work. The set ends with a powerful poem by Olzhas Suleimenov, an anti-nuclear activist from Kazakhstan.

Like writers before me, I am at something of a loss how to conclude this introduction. One aspect of Witherup's poetry, along with its meditation, its naturalness, its sensuality, and its emotional honesty, is (as James B. Hall has noted) its ability to capture "the complexity, the valence, the hysteria of being alone, of being up against it, of being driven by forces little understood."[2] Like Hall, I am not so surprised that Witherup has endured periods of breakdown and hospitalization as I am that his poetry has survived his pain. Make no mistake, the poetry is unrelenting. It shows us the madness of our world, our complicity in our own destruction, our seemingly pointless confusion of good and evil. It also names our enemies and calls its wrath down upon them. A Methodist as a young man, later a student of Eastern thought, Witherup seems to deliver a sermon (it may be Buddha's Fire Sermon), calling us to consciousness whether we want to be there or not. And he does this with the Devil's own humor.

This may be the one imperishable quality of art in the modern world. It makes us see despite ourselves. Truly a case of Root Hog or Die, as Witherup would have it.

John Crawford
August 1, 2000

1. Foreword, William Witherup, *Black Ash, Orange Fire: Collected Poems 1959–1985* (Point Reyes Station: Floating Island Publications, 1986), 14.

2. Afterword, *Black Ash, Orange Fire*, 216.

BEACONS, FABLES, MESSAGES

At Malya, Crete: 1959

We are a dream in the mind of God.
     —Spinoza

In a dream agony your image rises
from the bottom of my psyche,
rises like a sprig of pink coral fern
torn from a grotto in a sea swell,
rises to float upon my mind's surface
and troubles me from sleep.

Waking I hear the windmills turning
and, above the hissing swells,
bathers' laughter.
Often I dream a darker dream:
sunning or loving by the sea
our pleasure was another dreamer's pleasure.

Three Perspectives of San Francisco

from Sausalito

Is San Francisco at noon,
bright and flat against
a cerulean sky, a fresco
by Pierro della Francesca
or a projection of "The Beautiful"?
Sporting a florid shirt
the color of an infection,
a tourist is taking snapshots
from the boardwalk in Sausalito,
unaware his negatives are
of a sprawling, white hospital.

from Oakland

Is San Francisco at noon
white as the walls of Jerusalem
or white as the bones of blacks
bleached white in the African sun?
A stoned musician, standing
in an hotel doorway, knows:
as the sun fires his silver
alto sax he begins to blow—
"white buildings are facades
concealing kennels
where white hounds fatten
on crates of doves."

from Alcatraz

San Francisco at noon
is Venus rising from the sea
in a rush of sexual foam
to taunt the caged
with her white beauty.
What these pariahs see,
their faces pressed
against the wire mesh,
is missing in the vision
by Botticelli—
a nimbus of black light
surrounding her white flesh.

—1961

To a Salesgirl in Juarez

She stood in the cool shaft
of a gift shop doorway, her dress
morning glory blue against brown skin.
Her presence loosened the chrome yellow light
and the afternoon expanded, touching each man
in the plaza with the spaciousness
and destiny of a conquistador.

I travel with her still through personal deserts,
my water bag filled with the elixir of her smile,
for even the lizards are sick
of seeing the black, swollen tongues of poets.

—1964

In a Country of Warehouses

I dreamed
I was a stranger
in a country of warehouses
where the sun beat hard
against concrete slabs
and the doors
were as large
as cathedral doors

Inside
in darkness
men moved about slowly
like priests
among the pallets
of cocoa beans
stacked drums
of peanut oil
racks
of copper tubing

Some carried cargo hooks
that flashed
in their hands
like holy rings

I found the hooks
had several uses
There
in the harsh afternoon
workers
gutted me
like a chicken
to tear out
whatever it was
they feared

They found
a black jewel
and
an ovum

These
made them
furious

—*San Francisco, 1965*

Freeway

An infected vein
carrying filth to and from the city;

a funnel
draining a huge operating table.

Even the light here
is the color of pus.

All the late model cars
have tinted windows to shield the murderers

and the chrome is honed
to slash and carve.

And the city has drawn
a rubber curtain of shrubbery

to enclose the view
and muffle the screams.

—*Berkeley, 1966*

A Fable

When antelope first saw Men—
hairless, on their hind legs,
moving in a line across the veld—
a new terror ran in the animal's veins.

The lions, watching from the bush,
did not like the smell and slipped away.

But the hyenas were pleased
at the arrival of the Upright Ones,
and rolled ecstatically
in vomit and rotting meat

—*San Francisco, 1966*

Messages from a Zuni Fetish

1

An alabaster bear
with a turquoise arrowhead
strapped to its back with sinew
stands on my writing desk.

On fortunate days
the desk becomes an altar
covered with plume wands
and *tablitas* of clouds, lightning and corn.

When I open my ledger to write
it crumbles like an old parfleche bag.

2

Each night Zunis creep through my room
with drawn bows
to kill the albino grizzly
who has his will of their corn fields,
rifling the largest and sweetest ears.

The warriors' odor
mingles with the milky scent of corn;
the moonlight on the corn tassels
and on the plumed tassels of the bows
is like music.

I would like to reach out
and touch the nearest man on the arm,
but a stronger love goes out to the bear
and I snap a stalk to frighten him.

The Zunis turn and look at me
as if they'd known of my presence all the while.
I search for words to explain what I have done
and why I am there,
but the men slip away
into the deep shadows of the corn rows.

3

I come disguised as the Plumed Serpent,
my raft moving over black obsidian waters.
With the wind and moonlight in my feather cape
I feel as strong as a white-breasted sea eagle.

Montezuma waits on the steps of his palace,
arms outstretched to receive me, like a lover.
His wrists are adorned with gold bracelets;
his hair scented and oiled.

He trembles and looks uncertain
as he notices my blue eyes
and the paleness of my skin,
which is as white as holy wafers.

In my sash is a thin obsidian knife.
I slip it easily beneath his ribs
and sew myself and my kind
to the heart of the continent.

—*San Francisco, 1966*

Columbia River Suite

The Glacier

At one of its sources the river
is a field of ice
spilling into the Pacific.

At fourteen I was a passenger
on the *S. S. Alaska*—enroute to Seward.
We passed the glacier
from one mile out.
The captain slowed the ship,
and as his engineers blew the whistle
tall ice columns
splintered into the sea.

At thirty years I'm travelling nowhere,
except to work five days a week,
an irritable passenger, like the rest.
On its route down Market Street
the bus passes stores and offices,
where windows of black ice
hold people frozen in postures of despair.

Today my lunchbox froze to my side
and I looked at my reflection
and the faces of the others
for a sign, an illumination, a flame—
some demonstration of love to melt the ice.

2

The *S. S. Alaska* cuts dark water.
We pass a glacier of blue ice.
Standing on deck
I feel the glacier's cold breath.

I have been here before, another century,
a boy paddling a cedar canoe.
The old men have sent me out alone
to discover my spirit.
I have fasted and paddled two days,
the canoe drawn north by a strong force,
like a salmon after a feathered lure

When I find I am near Ice Mountain
hair freezes to my neck and my arms tighten.
But I face the mountain,
alert and still as a hunted rabbit,
sniffing the sharp air
and listening to the shift and snap of ice.

The Spirit of the ice sees me
and sits in my mouth, like a dead man's teeth.
Then Land Otter slides quickly over the bow.
I feel his wet fur on my back
as he chews my hair.
Then he whispers a song
and hangs an amulet around my neck.

I tap the paddle against the canoe
and sing Ice Mountain my new song.
I see my ancestors writhing
like larvae in the mountain's belly.

I am to be a singer.
I will return to my village
and make up songs
about the old age of the earth
and our swift journeys beneath the stars.

The Salmon Festival

1

At Celilo Falls the Columbia
broke to a lather of water and light,

and the salmon, shooting from pools and shelves,
flashed like silver reflectors.

That day I had a vision
that the salmon would be my totem.

I am lost now in a polluted slough,
seeking a channel to white water.

2

The old chief was buckskinned in white;
he had braided silver hair.
He filled the longhouse with light
as he blessed and praised the river.

The river has been dammed
and the old man is buried now.
I bow to his burial canoe—
praise the brightness of the prow.

3

In the longhouse
six men around a large drum
singing:
of silver white salmon
of flashing water
of glistening stones
of white nylon nets
of sharp white gulls
of white cranes in mist
of small white flowers
and:
of the shell-white East
of the moon as polished white shell
of the Original Path as crushed white shell

Listen!
the drum is calling the Ancient Ones
Their white moccasins glide along the path
They stand now on the far bank
in the wet grass
singing quietly to the salmon

Across from Celilo Falls
For Jim Scoggin

Above Goldendale we sat on a power relay tower
and sketched the fences and roads
that ran through ochre fields of stubble.
We drove away with the next year's harvest
shifting in our heads—
the grain flashing like hard kernels of light.

As the car whined into the gorge
salmon entered our blood,
searching for secret channels.
That night, driving home through ghostly sage
we felt them swimming upstream
to spawn millions of eggs in our hearts.

Across the river from the falls we ate lunch
on a flat, grassy bank. Beneath the grass
rock sank its shafts deeply in the riverbed
and we felt the river sliding past the rock,
the cold, abrasive water working it.
We lay in the grass, propped on our elbows,
drinking pop, smoking,
watching the river in the afternoon light.

When we found the glyphs of fish, deer and sun
on the nearby rocks, our forehead were marked
with signs, our temples pulsed like drum skins
and we danced.
We danced and sang *The Dance of the White Deer.*

The Great White Father

Engineers
found the Great White Father dying,
caught in a fish ladder at the Dalles.
He wore a rubber mask
that disguised him as an Indian grandmother
and his last words were,
"I want to be loved!"

After two centuries massacring
salmon and buffalo on the dark river floor,
he had tried to climb to the light.

The medicine man summoned
to sing for the Great White Father's shadow
had a vision of it slipping down river
towards Portland
bloated with ears and testicles
and human hair.

—*San Francisco, 1966*

Depression

My mattress floats in an ocean of newspapers
through the eternal night of the fifty states.
On the ocean floor generals and editors
ride sharks through forests of sea anemones,
sabreing Sioux and Blacks and Vietnamese.

I try desperately to sleep, to dream—
anything to shut out the hissing sound
of limbs and heads as they bob to the surface
from fathomless layers of print.
Any moment I expect my daughters' heads.

—*San Francisco, 1967*

After My Breakdown

After my breakdown
I tried Compōz.
I went back to Brylcream.
I joined the Dodge Rebellion
and the Pepsi Generation.
I flew the friendly skies of United.
I put a tiger in my tank.
I ate the Breakfast of Champions.

After my first relapse
I filled my cupboard with Wonderbread,
my icebox with the beer beer drinkers drink.
I packed into Marlboro country
sporting a fresh tattoo.
I arrested death and decay with Macleans.
I killed body odors with Jade East.
I fought despair #100 with Excedrin
and pain #200 with Anacin
and anxiety #600 with Contac.

After my second relapse I cured myself
with Gillette stainless steel blades.

On the Death of Theodore Roethke

The papers say he died in a swimming pool,
but that is not the way poets go.
A poet's exit is terrible: as his hour
approached the wind began to blow,
rattling the windows of his study.
Below the lake shuddered; fish went still.
Above the light soured like spoiled grapefruit.
He listened and heard the awful rupture
of petals and stems and a chorus of worms
singing in the compost. He laid down his pen
and went out, feeling the weight of his flesh,
sensing his time of singing was done,
he who had turned the world into honey.
And he moved through his garden like a heavy bee,
his dark suit gathering a bloody pollen.

—Santa Fe-San Francisco, 1964–1966

For a Still-Born Niece

A thousand miles from you, sister,
I plunge my wrists in the ocean
until they are braceleted with salt.
Then I raise them to the sun
as beacons for the child's soul.

—*San Francisco, 1966*

We Were Each Alone

En estas soledades estuviste:
Paris es un desierto para la timidez de los recien llegados.
            —Enrique Lihn

We were each alone:
San Francisco is a desert to the shyness of love.
You sat in a rocking chair by the window,
wanting to die. The streetlight on the corner
shone on your face and bathrobe with the bluish-whiteness
of desert moonlight. I looked in your eyes
and the pupils were as wide as a Saharan night.
You were not in the room, but were walking among ruins,
trailing a broken wing.

I followed you and came to the desert of my self,
where sand and sky blazed a harsh light.
I asked my shadow for a prophecy
and it vomited three black yolks.
At the oasis a headless statue of Eros
was bleeding in stagnant water.
I walk now among dying camels
carrying a photograph of your eyes.

—1967

Saida

Your body, turning lightly in bed,
is a lighted ship moving in a dark bay
and contains the mystery of night and distance.
As you dock, knocking softly against me,
my skin reflects your lights
and our talk becomes the estranged voices
of passengers.

Your body, turning lightly in bed,
is a white Arabian mare
wheeling in the desert night.
The small bells in your mane
fill the room with music.

Your body, turning lightly in bed,
glows in the moonlight like plankton.
Wherever I touch you there is a radiance,
as of a night swimmer in a phosphorescent sea.
Beneath your skin there shines another light,
a sea anemone whose interior
is the electric green of pool tables.

I enter you in search of the ocean floor,
a unicorn cutting his flesh on the coral.

—*San Francisco, 1965*

Siren—Woman and Bird

In a small bed we tried the nights.
The sails were the violet of your pupils
and were scented with patchouli.
Your sex was a soft net
opening and closing in the tides
and I a drowned swimmer
brought up from the ocean floor
to where your fingers
pulled sea anemones from my spine
and my body bled
against the coral of your teeth.

Siren—woman and bird,
you have folded into yourself
in a sleep that excludes me.
My poems are fading charts,
useless for mapping the currents
that light your feet
and the hidden reefs
that explode in your hair.

—*San Francisco, 1966*

Marian at Tassajara Springs

1

I remember your hair
spread out like black moss against the rock,

your skin tasting faintly sulphurous
from the mineral baths,

your laughter like a spring
swelling up

from the lime and chalk of your pelvis
and flowing out the white stones of your teeth.

I caught the small trout of your tongue
in my mouth.

2

It was October.
The Monarchs were dying,

falling through the air
like oak leaves

and landing on the rocks and stones
where they would rest,

slowly moving their faded
orange and black wings

as if they were trying to fan themselves
back into flame.

We talked of the certain end
of our season

as the crumpled ghosts of old lovers
floated past us on the water,

and of something waiting
in cities and in each of us

that is hostile to love
and to rocks in clear streams.

I will think of that day
and the wings of your shoulders

when the firestorm comes
and the wind

whips my shirt
to black ash and orange flame.

—*San Francisco, 1967*

Marian/"Chama" in Three Mountain Ranges

1

Now we separate
branch letting go of pine cone.
On Tamalpais there is darkness,
mist and silence.

2

Are there daisies on the mountain now
and will we meet there again—
you to open to me from a white blouse
the gold cores of your nipples?

3

If you return to the spot on the mountain
where we ate slices of pineapple and watermelon,
say hello to the black ants who sucked
the sweet rinds and watched our lovemaking.

4

Woman of the mountains, touch me again
with your feet and hair.
Let me smell the pollen on your fingertips
and eat wildflower petals from your sex.

5

Your hair is as beautiful
as a black fern
preserved for eternity
deep in a mountain of ice.

6

The veins in your hand are the veins of a leaf
that is slowly changing to coal.
Someday your hand
will heat the roots of mountain flowers.

7

You have moods where you travel back to your
father's seed—to the pitiless sun of the Sierra
Madres. Your eyes harden to the obsidian of carved
serpents; then you would eat my steaming heart.

8

We made love in a sleeping bag beneath a full moon.
Now the moon is the upper jaw of a skull biting
the dirt, and the road through the Los Padres
is a powder of crushed bone.

9

A wild boar runs through the Los Padres
with your heart on his tusk.
Hopelessly I stuff moss and leaves
in the wound beneath your breast.

10

I have been searching for you
in the snows of the Sangre de Cristo.
Though I lost you only yesterday
I have grown old and snowblind.

—*San Francisco, 1968*

For a Lady Who Loves Schubert

After a week in Hell
we are suddenly driving a yellow Volvo
through the snow in New Mexico.

This is a fact—
I am not writing a surrealist poem
for *Sixties* or *kayak*—

we have spent seven days in Hell
with a Zen monk
who is as mad as the Karamazovs,
and now we are moving at sixty miles per hour
through snow and light
or, if you choose,
at six hundred miles per hour
through the pages of an absurd novel.

It is a wonderful vacation:
we have brought our suffering with us.
Through sunglasses—greath cthonic masks—
we stare tragically into the harsh light,
Oedipus and Medea
bleeding in the small orchestra
of a foreign car,
while outside a chorus of Penitentes
flagellate themselves in the snow.

To the poet's noble profile
you offer a story from *True Secrets:*
HE ONLY WANTED ME NAKED.
You give me so much pleasure
that I am suddenly smacked with joy
and I ask you to pass me the Joy Stretchers.

You are a hard bitch
for a lady who loves Schubert.

—*Santa Fe-San Francisco, 1967*

Hybrid Villanelle on a Line by Li Po

Drunk on the moon, a sage of dreams,
I offer the mountain a shot of bourbon,
and I offer you a shot from the hip.

The last full moon I called you on the phone,
drunk on the moon, a sage of dreams,
and talked to a cloud your ear.

Tonight clouds move across the moon
and I write this poem by candlelight,
drunk on the moon, a sage of dreams.

Drunk on the moon, a sage of dreams,
I pick up the phone to dial your hair
but the line is dead, the mouthpiece a crater.

Two moths have snuffed out in the candle flame.
Drunk on the moon, a sage of dreams,
my moth heart crackles in the lunar fire.

You are probably making love tonight,
giving your Zen monk rice wine from the hip.
Drunk on the moon, a sage of dreams,
I piss a bloody stain in the moonwhite dirt.

—*Santa Fe, 1968*

A Day of Scattered Rain

It is a day of scattered rain.
A wind, blowing from the direction
of the Sangre de Cristos,
carries the scents of wet cedar and juniper,
of damp earth and sand,
and mixes it with the perfumes
of blossoming apricot, cherry and peach.

A thousand miles and two months away
and I am still disturbed
by these metaphors of your skin.
Nose, pores and heart
are overloaded with memories of your smell.
I have become a cloud
swollen with blossoms and moisture—
the pain of left-over love.

Take me, wind, over the mountains
and let me break open!

—*Santa Fe, 1968*

AMERICAN DREAMS AND SHADOW PLAYS

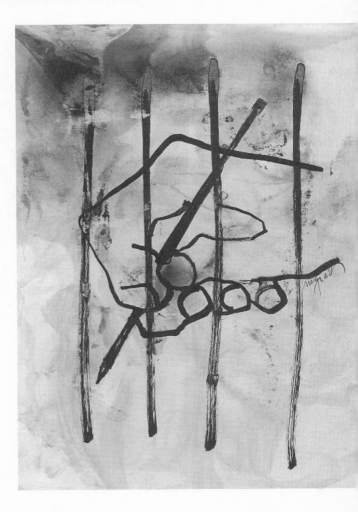

A Man's Life

The life of man is like a shadow play
Which must in the end return to nothingness
    —T'ao Ch'ien (365–472)

The grasses and wild asters
wave in the wind.
The jays are flashes of blue flame
in the pine trees.

I have just finished a bowl of Quaker Oats
with fresh apricots and raisins
and am drinking green tea
on the cabin porch.

At 33 the poet T'ao Ch'ien
gave up courtly life
and went into the mountains
seeking the *Tao*.

Same age
I have come to this log cabin
where the wind sounds as if
it hones off a hill of skulls,

and the creek across the road
is the sound of the *Way*.
My past is 33 shadows
thrown swiftly on a screen.

—*Santa Fe, 1968*

Apricot Tree

For the poet Beverly Dahlen

1

Sitting on the cabin porch
watching the stars and drinking wine with a friend,
I am suddenly aware of the slow, black
gnarled fountain of the apricot tree.

2

Oh blue jay in the apricot tree
aren't you afraid your feathers will catch fire
and your eyes burn out
in those galaxies of red-orange suns?

3

In the rain
the leaves of the apricot tree
are turning dark green.

There is large thunder over the mountains
and the small thunder of apricots
on the cabin roof.

—Santa Fe, 1968

On a Dead Swallow

Here you are, grounded in road gravel,
that yesterday flashed in and out of eaves,
your orange breast flaring like a coal,
your tail two columns of blue smoke.

I witness the transmutation of fire
as your flight passes like a shadow
into the swarm of black ants
that move in frenzy over your feathers.

Now they are burrowing around the eye,
mining it like precious metal,
saving the gold disc until the last
to raise up gloriously from your bones.

—*Santa Fe, 1968*

At Jeannie's in El Rito

There are simple pleasures—
such as drawing water from a well
next to a field where eight goats
are grazing,
and an ancient Spanish goat man
forks alfalfa.

2

Sometimes there is as much anger
in loving as love.
Feeling blacker than fish guts
I leave her
for a walk in the early morning light,
and pick a torch of wildflowers
to cut through my hatred.

—1968

Rito

Short for El Rito. The town dog.
Ate handouts, everybody's friend
until deliberately run over by drunk teenagers;
then became Jeannie's, who picked him up,
large as he was, and took him home.

They broke his back, but not his spirit.

We brought him to my place,
hoping he would heal.
Each day he dragged himself down to the creek
two hundred yards from the cabin—
and I always had to fetch him and carry him
back up, muddy and stinking.

He wouldn't be still; refused to be sick;
kept challenging dogs and horses.
The sores on his hind legs spread,
ate through hair and meat—
until they found bone.
Then we knew.

I dug him a shallow grave by the creek,
with bare hands and a stick,
so that I could get closer to his death
while Jeannie fed him
a last meal, mixed with sleeping pills.
Then I carried him down and laid him in.

Shot him between the eyes with a .22—
and as his head jerked forward on his paws,
his soul rushed past us
and it dropped me to my knees, my hat off,
and our tears were copious and hot

for Rito, the town dog—a free spirit!

—*El Rito, 1968*

Aspen Ranch Road

1

The light snow is silver on the road.
The moon is a cuticle of ice.
The rose hips are frozen drops of blood.
The stream falls coldly over the rocks.
All of nature is clearly etched this morning.
Even my pain, which is as black
as the tire tracks cutting the snow.

2

The aspens and birches
are dying into themselves.
The buds are closed
like small fists.
This time of year
we grow harder.
Our bones assert themselves
over flesh.
They shine inside us
cold and white
as naked birches.

—*Santa Fe, 1968*

An American Dream

The Paiute in Modesto
talked of his new orange tractor
and of his peaches ripening.
We walked out to see his orchards,
shielding our eyes against the light,
to find the branches crusted with maggots
and the fruit dripping.
"America, America, America," he wept.
As I put my arm around his shoulders
the darkness rushed in,
leaving us in an empty field by a freeway.
It trembled and we knew we had to cross.
We stepped over the shoulder,
our faces clay masks beneath the blue arcs,
and the freeway closed behind us
with the faint whirring of a theater curtain.
As we walked into the darkness
the gourd rattles of the Eternal Ones
began to sound the night, like crickets.

—*San Francisco, 1968*

Coast Live Oak

The oak is old
and arthritic
with gallnuts

Its limbs are bearded
with wisps of lichen

An ancient
bird's nest
rests on a bony branch

My hand
rests
on its gray skin

For we want communion
across
the illusion of form

There are no words
for how deeply
I love this tree

—Palo Colorado Canyon, 1969

Two from the Monterey Hotel

1: Let's Raise a Glass of Port to the Old Caddy

Didn't know much about the old guy.

Face flushed the color of port,
dressed in gold cap and wind-breaker.

Had a friendly word for you,
but stayed in his room most of the time,
cuddling his pint of Gallo.

Remembering, maybe, the greens,
the flags; breakers off Cypress Point.

And then they brought in the motorized carts . . .

We found him recently dead.
Fully dressed,
curled up fetally on the bed,
pool of brown vomit and mucus on the pillow.

His only angels a box of soda crackers
and a carton of sour milk.

Had to help the coroner
Carry the stretcher down stairs.

Tibbits, a small man, but heavy at death,
weighing as much as two full golf bags.

2: Portrait of a Desk Clerk

She takes as long as a Kabuki actor making up,
fitting on first black lacquer wig,
then false eyelashes and violet nails.
Pats on cologne and baby powder
until the halls have a sweetish stink.
While she elaborates her costume she hums,
merrily, but tunelessly, *dee dee dum dum*.

She hums for me a few doors down
painting over piss stains and despair
with Fashion Tone.
She hums for the alcoholic down the hall
who thinks he is in love with her.
She hums for the whole third floor,
letting them know this dump won't get *her* down.

She's made up a story about an estate.
When it's settled, she'll be in the chips.
I nod when I hear it again, to help her believe.
She's going to do something worldwide for kids
and will hire me at four bucks an hour.

With a final flourish of Lemon Mist
She signs out of her room
and descends to her estate.

—*Monterey, 1969*

Portola Cannery Poem

Bells ring furiously
summoning us on deck.
The boss's old sea turtle face
rises from deep water.
We are about to get orders
to murder five million squid
for the gourmet tables
of the Greek dictator.

Already the bay is stained with ink.
Rusty gears, levers and chain-link belts
begin their slow grinding below.
I am ashamed of my part in this.
I throw my M-1 in the water.
I want to dive into the ink
and disappear forever,
like a drowned man
in a medieval drawing.

—*Cannery Row, 1969*

The Soledad Prison Poems

Driving to Class

1

Driving through the Salinas Valley
lettuce fields
I pass pickets
of the United Farm Workers.

Red flags
stamped with the black Aztec eagle
snap in the wind
above flashing teeth
and raised brown fists.

Near Gonzales a crow
swings in a hangman's noose
from a telephone line.
It hexes the field of a grower
who has bussed in scab labor
from Arizona.

A few miles further
the huge prison smokestack
points its yellow snout
at the sky.

2

Eighty miles south, at Salmon Creek,
chaparral, oak, greasewood and pine
explode in the heat.
White ashes drift on Monterey,
and the sun is a diseased pink.

"It's as bad as the fire bombing
of Dresden," one man says.
The fire boss remarks,
"The hardest part for us is chasing
the burning animals back into the fire."

At Soledad bureaucrats
flap wet shirts; guards
drink beer and piss in the cells.
Burning prisoners fall back,
the world still safe from crime.

And where are you going, teacher,
in your lettuce green suit and new cordovans?
Turn around, break into flame.
Leap from the car
and run down the freeway,
scorched with the pain of birth and death.

Full Moon Over Soledad

The light of a full moon
falls on the prison.

Guards keep watch in the towers,
licking the oil from shotguns
with their lizard tongues.

Prisoners' hands reach out
of the barred windows,
thirsting for the pure
silver water of the moon.

Now and then a hand leaves
and flies away
like the wing of an owl.

Upstairs in the Education Wing

Upstairs in the Education Wing
we are rapping about the death
of *Psyche* in prison.
Each man is quiet, each thoughtful.
Tonight we are together
and it is beautiful.

Nearing the end of class
we hear shouts below.
Men are rioting in O-Wing,
burning sheets and blankets,
sending up smoke signals from Hell.

After class,
walking the long corridor
of the Main Line, I pass O Wing.
Through the small window
in the heavy metal door
I see guards in gas masks
and yellow slickers scurrying
through the smoke and tear gas.

They are mutant locusts
laying eggs in the dead.

Elegy for George Jackson

1

They say you died in a patch of sunlight.
After ten lightless years.
Gunned down from behind.
Black man running through the woods
for two hundred years.
Gunned down by the sheriff.
Strung up and burned by the Klan.
Gunned down by the tower guard.
Gunned down running through the alley
toward that patch of light,
that open space where you might breathe
at last.

I hope it is true
that you died in the sun,
that at least they are not lying
about that.

Bless the grass that sponged your blood.
Bless the ant that drank from your tears.
Bless your mother's pillow
that has turned to a block of salt.

2

Perhaps you don't need these words
from a white man,
but I tape them on the wall anyway
and stand in the shadows as you sprint by.
I am cheering you toward that patch of light.
This time you will make it.
Beyond the wall.
Beyond the fence.

To that open space the sheriff can't see,
that the deputy can't see,
that the realtor can't see—
because the light is blinding
and the boundaries are intangible.

3

Your brothers are weeping, George.
This is the hour of lamentation.
This is the hour when the gun towers
turn into flaming pillars to mark your way,
and the barbed wire into harp strings.
This is the hour of our desire.
The worms cover your skin with mica
in preparation for your ascension.
With Che and Malcolm
you enter the hour of myth.

Road to the Yellow Prison

1

"Are you going
to *Souldead* tonight?"
Asked Carmen's youngest, Tony.
Yes.
To *Soul Dead*.
Along
the River Road
at dusk
in early spring
in the solitude
of a battered
'53 Ford
through the lettuce capital
of the world.
To *Soul Dead*
a journey that should be made

on foot
that should end
with me falling
on my knees
like Father Zossima
and kissing a murderer's feet
because of what
I have learned of suffering

there
without suffering
myself
because Americans
hide their suffering
hide their death
in prisons
in mental institutions
in foreign wars
and will not
fall down and weep—
the cold blue-eyed
Anglo Saxons
Of whom
I
am one.

2

Soledad.
Spanish word
for loneliness
for solitude
dark syllables
of the dreaming
earth
in the shadows
of The Pinnacles
a spot where
if there were
no prison there
a man might go
to speak
to his *Shadow Self.*

But the spirit
is twisted
in the House
of the Dead.
There a man
may not fall down
in the perfumed
grasses of spring
and nourish
his *Shadow Self*
his female self.
And looking for
the woman
in himself
he spills his semen
and his blood
on concrete.

Goes insane
inside what is
called
a Correctional
Training Facility.

3

After class
I get in
my sarcophagus—
my limestone coffin.
This is my
ship to the sun,
my stone boat
out of the galaxy.
But it does not float.
Instead
it grates
back and forth
the River Road
four nights
a week
towed by
twenty skeletons
hauling on ropes
of prisoner hair.

4

When friends
ask me how
I like teaching
at the prison
I open my mouth
and show
them a tongue
of sulfur yellow
dust
and two rows
of stone maggots
for teeth.

—*Monterey, 1970–71*

Robert Bly at Point Lobos

Day after Bly and Ferlinghetti
visited Soledad with me

While I study the red blisters
of lichen on the dying cypress,
he scribbles furiously in the rain,
trying to capture the spirit
of rocks in a smoking sea.

With his clear plastic raincoat
billowing like a fish bladder,
like a bag of waters,
I seem him as he truly is—
a stranger, risen among us
from a watery life.

—*Point Lobos, 1970*

Night: Soberanes Point

At the ocean my nose
was full of salt air.
Now on the path back
to the car I notice
the female scent of lilac
mixed with male odors
of horsemint and sage.

As I lean over to break
a sprig of lilac
my flashlight finds
a golden poppy,
its petals folded
like a nesting yellow bird.

I switch off the light
and look up at the sky,
that dark unfolding flower
filled with rushing, burning
star anthers.

O blossoming night!

—*Big Sur, 1971*

To the President of the Company

that produces pop-top cans;
to the president of the corporation
turning out plastic rings
for six-packs;
and the president of the conglomerate
that manufactures disposable diapers—

give them each an eight foot gunnysack
and a stick with a nail in it;
have them walk this coast
in their suits and ties,
stabbing trash and stuffing sacks
until they trail behind
like bloated instestines.

Give them no mercy,
only water and bread,
and let a garbage truck
follow them
so they can empty the sacks.

Yes, they may sleep at night,
but curled up on the roadbed
with only their gunnysacks for cover.

Show them no mercy.
Make them walk and pick
until their faces are blistered,
and their fine suits
stained and ragged,
until their toes burst from their shoes.

May they walk the rest of their lives
in shame, hiding their faces from the stars.

—*Big Sur, 1971*

John Haines

Opens and shuts doors in stone.

Lopes down from a blue glacier,
head black against the sunset's orange fire,
dark mouth prophesying.

John. John the Baptist.
Grasshoppers and honey.
Shaman. Mad monk in seal fur.
Drinker of melted snow.

Gives songs to the wind.
Combs ferns with a bone.

Talking of Yeats.
Talking of John Clare.
Drinking rum from a mountain goat's horn.

An abcess in his tooth,
an edginess.

A voice with boulders in it, rumbling.

Songs made of basalt
And owls' blood.

—Monterey, 1971

Mojave

In a time of drought her name was River.
After a month of rain I name her Mojave.

She brushes my face with a hawk-wing fan
and offers a breast crusted with black salt.

The flies have taught me how to mourn her;
cicadas, the dry sound of loss.

Sentence follows sentence into the desert
where wind erases her scent and my words.

Memory of her neck and the mucous of thighs
lures me to the entrance of the magnetite mine.

It is blocked by windrows of lice;
termites foam in the dead timbers.

In the mine shaft Chemehuevi chant a death song
about white men who prospect for dark women.

Behind me Kelso dune shrieks and booms her name,
and its quartz crystals grind an ominous light.

—*Big Sur, 1972*

Yucca

Hiking with Carmen

Our Lord's Candle
bursts from the granite mountain.
Honeybees fling themselves
in and out of its sweet waxy flowers.

I climbed to it from a field of lupine,
a field of blue fire,
thinking no further beauty was possible
this spring morning on the trail.

And now this yucca seething with bees,
this harp cracking the mountain
with a continual hum.

—*Big Sur, 1972*

Frost

The air condenses
during the night

leaving a shine
on the ferns and grasses.

It is like silver pollen
glimmering in a dream.

When the sun flashes
over the ridge

I dance into my cold jeans
and step outside

to go for a walk
in a lake of pure light.

—*Bixby Creek, 1972*

Alders

Growing in moist earth
by the creek,

pulling coolness down
into the canyon,

platinum in the early
morning,

silver
in the afternoon,

becoming then more
buoyant,

floating upwards
on the light,

flashing
in the wind,

making another music
counterpoint

to the flowing
of water.

At dusk
the trees turn inward,

listening
to themselves.

The saw-toothed leaves
eat darkness,

chew a wound
in the sky

and a deep violet oil
seeps downward.

It is then the alders
call me outside

to stand on the large
cabin porch

listening to the electric
charge of the night breeze,

the nearest alder tossing,
sighing,

like a body being swept
by dreams.

—*Bixby Creek, 1972*

Gathering Wood for the Winter

The soft rasp of a bow saw
spilling dust on the horsemint.
Sweat, flies and this fallen tree;
the bitter oil of crushed nettles
and the living alders
breathing the morning light.

Back at the woodpile
milk foams around the steel wedge
and the halved logs startle
with their whiteness
like split loaves of fresh bread.

—*Bixby Creek, 1973*

For the Alders Again

Each morning your branches
flung wide in welcome
to a friend you have known
for millions of years.

Out getting wood again
I draw my bow across
the bones of your dead
and play saw music.

The morning light flashes
from leaf to leaf
from leaf to saw
and back to leaf.

I am a blessed man.
I shine in a new skin of sweat
as I lift in my arms
your great spinal discs.

—*Bixby Creek, 1973*

Going Up for the Mail

1

Walking up for the mail,
Sobaka in front of me
scattering quail,
snuffling the freshest holes.
Then he breaks through a beam
of deer scent, wheels
and splashes through again and again.
Each time he crosses a jet
he triggers the secret path
that only the deer know.
And it drives him nuts,
because he can never find it.

2

A spot on the road
blisters with small volcanoes.
Black wasps simmer in the cores,
eyes and stingers lava-red.
They are so mad with life and fire
they erupt and fling out
to burn the world,
setting the first blaze
on Sobaka's ass.

—*Bixby Creek, 1973*

Winter Darkness

*The same cabin where Kerouac wrote that
very poor book, "Big Sur"*

Rain and the roadbank
weeping red breccia.

Oak ashes flaking in the fireplace—
seconds of Eternity.

The termite is back,
scooping and grinding behind my eyes.

I pour slow shots of Jim Beam
in the rotten wood to wash him out.

Winter darkness comes early,
slashing across the cabin like a rock slab.

—Big Sur, 1972

Thinking about Suicide

The far cold stars above Big Sur,
the moon a cyanide tablet,
freezing the night to white crystal,
filling it with the odor of bitter almonds.
My shadow follows me down the road,
leaking from my boot heels like blood.

—*Big Sur, 1972*

Sphinx Moth

Written on the eve of poet Eric Barker's death

A moth the size of a hummingbird
that flew in last night
and filled our evening with shadows.

Hovering, feverish, beating now
against the glass. I study
the feathery hairs on its thorax,

the smoked eyes, the secret
pink underwing that wounds me
like an insane child's mouth.

I cup the moth's hot life in my hand,
open the window and give it
to the morning, to the bare alders,

to its destiny. It leaves behind
a fluttering pulse in my palm
and a silky smear from another world.

—*Bixby Creek, 1972*

Death Is Behind Us

Death is behind us
with his brights on.
The inside of the car
is lit up like a poisonous flower.

The kids are fighting again.
An owl's bloody beak
chatters under the seat.

Carmen is weeping
because I have blunt fingers.
I am crying because
I can not turn off the road—
because I am frozen in *Father.*

—*Bixby Creek, 1972*

Hornet's Nest

This huge bubble of chewed wood
hanging from a single twig
over Bixby Creek

This decapitated mummy head
wrapped in gray cloth
breathing yellow striped hornets

This death mask
with its soft buzzing song
its primordial tune

of instinctual life
makes me want to beat
it furiously with a stick

—*Bixby Creek, 1973*

At the Sign of the Fish

The man with fish blood
streaming down his knuckles
kneels by the creek.
The rainbow, gold hook
tearing its gullet,
vomits juices,
the stippled light
of its roses fading
with each heartbeat.

Light passes into the man
and hooks his belly.
Anger comes up like bile
and mixes with
the salts of love.

He tilts his knife
at the evening sky,
wipes the crust of blood
and scales
on his pants,
stands in the creek thinking,
waiting for darkness.

—*Bixby Creek, 1973*

Five Fractured Preludes for Blue Bear

For Steve Taugher

1

Dear friend, I envy your fields of blue snow,
wolves singing at the edge of your farm,
moose horns black against the moon.
So I send you what winter news I have,
a few tracks against this paper's white field.

2

Our first winter storm today.
One thousand smoking mountains at the beach
and crackling glaciers of green ice.
Grandfather rocks coughing in their icy beards.
The brine on my lips is the salt of joy.

3

Sat in my pickup this morning
just listening to the rain on the cab,
inhaling the stew of bayleaves and mud.
That's all.
Sobaka kept looking at me.
He thought we were going somewhere.

4

Borrowed a pack of smokes from downroad neighbor.
Smoking and listening to Schubert
between the wild bars of music in the alders.
Franz Schubert died at thirty-one,
fatally in love with water and darkness.
Myself, I walk on surfaces, in too much light.

5

The Navajos swept down the plains
between the Rockies and the coast,
bringing with them the deadly arctic bow.
Sing for me their faces in the winter winds
and sing of your own boot tracks in the snow
next time you go out to milk the cows.

—*Bixby Creek, 1972*

Moonwatching and Steelhead

The moon rises over the ridge,
a chunk of milky quartz
set in a basalt sky.

Some nights the creek is dark wine.
Tonight it is clear gin
and I am drunk on it.

Monlight sifts down
through the dark crystals
in the cobalt waves.

It strikes steelhead
waiting at the creek mouth
for the winter rains.

They love the moonlight.
How they shine in it,
gills winking like hot coals.

A moonless night
weeks from now
I will walk the creek,

my life glowing with their gift—
a thousand moons
shining from underwater stones.

—*Bixby Creek, 1972*

Crows

I love crows.
If I met one human size
I would invite him into my living room
and offer him the softest chair.
Then we would crack a fifth of *Old Human*
and talk late into the night.
The room would be filled
with the shine and rustle of his feathers
and the wit of his sharp eye.

Prayer for a Young Gray Fox

For Joe Bruchac and an unknown woman driver

You made the night for Joe and me,
had run into the front tire of another car
and were stunned on the highway,
dark blood-flowers at your muzzle.

If all the beasts were gone, Chief Sealth said
in a letter to President Franklin Pierce,
men would die from great loneliness of spirit.

The driver, a woman, was kind enough to stop,
did not know what to do, asked our help.
The three of us bent down to watch over you
in the great loneliness of the coast night.
Your gaze was so clear we could not speak.

*Whatever happens to the beast also happens
to man. All things are connected. Whatever
befalls the sons of earth . . .*

We kept vigil, two sons, one daughter of earth;
decided you were shocked, had only a bloody nose;
helped you off the highway with thick gloves
to protect against your hunter's teeth.

*We might understand if we knew what it was
that the white man dreams, what hopes
he describes to his children on winter nights,
what visions he burns into their minds.*

May you, fox who runs through my dreams now,
your tail floating joyously above the chaparral,
carry in your memory three human faces
who loved you a December night.

—*Coast Highway, Big Sur, 1973*

DOWN CREEK, UP HOLLER

October in Appalachia

The last katydid knocks its tambourine,
dancing me here into what dark dream?
A bloody cloth is wiped across the trees
and the hills are full of howling strays.

Coal trucks hauling tons of darkness run
from Quicksand and Hazard and Kingdom Come,
dragging huge roots on underground chains,
leaking inky water thick as caulking.

This rocky shoulder leans toward winter sun.
The delicate mosses pray, gripping stone,
and broken dulcimers break into flame.
The stars press our bones into what black seam?

—*Hindman, Kentucky, 1973*

Reading High School Poems in Hindman, Kentucky

For the novelist-poet James Still

After exhaustion,
after days of talking about poetry,
hating my glib tongue and performer's mask,
I came across a student poem
that brought me to love again.

It was like returning from a journey
to find my house lit up,
fresh bread and coffee waiting
and a woman standing by the chair
smiling and saying *Welcome, welcome
and how was your trip?*

Then rubbing my shoulders while I ate.

—*Hindman, 1973*

Dog Dying

Dog dying in the hot sun.
Dog dying on a sheet of bloody leaves.
Crippled by car and dog fight,
rolled off the road shoulder to the creek.
Hind legs gnawed by muskrats,
wearing a seething mask of flies.

Dog dying, barking all night through my sleep,
barking for solace
against his bloody going,
a fever of maggots in his skull.

Dying there in the clear noon light,
the stink of him a smoke in the air.

We bathed him, we gave him water;
we might have kissed his sores,
who reminded us of our fragility
and the mortality of nerves and meat.

—Hindman, 1973

On Campus in Kentucky

For the poet Richard Taylor

This huge maple lifts its rosy flame
among the red brick buildings.
Leaves sputter in the breeze,
spark and drift off.
I place my hands on the black, wet bole
and bleed into the bark.
The tree bleeds into the lines of my palms
and I am raised up in the hissing branches
above the Sunday traffic.
I can hear the atoms burning in the bricks,
rose-gray ashes drifting from cornices.

—Frankfort, 1973

Dream during First Snow Storm

On this winter night a dream of Susan,
a dream of bird and tree and fire.
Cardinal, red as a gout of blood,
spread its wings and was turning,
turning in a field of snow.

Then it was Susan, with unbound hair,
whirling in a scarlet nightgown.
As she danced the icy walnut trees
cracked open, each to its lava core.
The only sound was lava
hissing and spitting in the snow.

I woke, in the ashes of my sheets,
to a cold wind in the power lines.

—*Frankfort, 1977*

How the Jilted Lover Spends His Time

Reading, finally, *Madame Bovary*
and *The Tao of Physics.*
Pacing the floor.
Smoking Camels.
Listening to the traffic,
the trains, and the wind.
Hearing words flake off the blackboards
in emergency classrooms.
Kneading balls of blood and shit
and throwing them at the calendar.
Avoiding sleep and its attendant dreams.
Searching for the lost dog of humor
(last seen bloated in the Kentucky River).
Ironing my jester suit.
Writing the word *suicide* on the wall.
Mixing glaze for my clay penis.
Reading *Hustler* magazine on the toilet.
Shopping for Christmas presents
to celebrate the Christ child's death.
Writing mercury-filled letters to friends.
Broiling my heart in cosmic rays.
Sipping Yellowstone whiskey
in a bare limestone landscape.
Composing satiric, unfinished essays
on Women and the Unconcious.
Contaminating students
with phials of bubonic poetry.
Laughing hysterically
at the infantile bawling of Literary Careers.
Waiting for the call that never comes
and for the dry bone
of the telephone to crumble off the wall.

—*Frankfort, 1977*

Shawhan, Kentucky: Winter 1978

The trees explode outward
in bursts of frost,
scattering crows across the snow
like black seeds.

Icy fog smolders
on the farm houses.
Icicles glitter and crack
on eaves and gutters.

Even so
the farmer across the road
has let out his sows
to forage the crusted fields.

These will have none
of my winter despair.
They plough their snouts
in the snow and fiercely live.

Western Kentucky Farmer

For Julia Alvarez

He soaks his calloused hands
in steaming hog's blood.
Talks of naked girls in the barn;
has published a book
of doggerel about God and Heaven.
Baits Julia and me,
his poet-guests at supper,
with a story about the time
when he was a railroad fireman
and put a *nigger* in the firebox
between Chicago and Louisville—
"Didn't need a stick more firewood!"

Sixty years of hard labor;
fireman, mason, farmer, liar,
his face shoved together like an old boar's.
And *crafty eyed*—
delighting in himself and our discomfort
while his wife serves up,
winking at us conspiratorially,
dish after dish
of the *finest* Kentucky home cooking.

—*Mayfield, 1978*

Milling Redwood up Vicente Creek

We rise out of the old sawdust, like ghosts,
our hands bloody with redwood stain.

Gouts of fresh sawdust wash over us
from the pink-gold heart of the new log.

We jabber and joke and tease,
exhuberant at each true 4 x 8.

Frank, John, Robbie, Sam, Bill—
a brotherhood of men in honest labor,

dancing, as earth lurches around the sun,
to the vortices of knots; the nebulae of grain.

—*Big Sur, 1978*

To Bixby Creek Again,
and to You, Raccoon

Shocked awake
by the half-nail moon
jabbing deep into the canyon—
so bright I felt
an unnamed guilt in my gut.

Fell back to sleep
as the moon traced the sky.
Woke again near dawn
to your perfect footprint
on the misted window—
like burning lace.

Thanks, masked partner
and fellow poet
for sharing the night's crime,
whatever it was we did.

And let's not
let those bastards catch us.

—*Bixby Creek, 1980*

April Night

For Dian

The full moon is a blue rosebud
and the stars are distant chimes.
There is the rustle of bird wings
in the eaves, flame roaring in the wood stove.
Our daughters are dreaming
and perhaps you are dreaming, pregnant lady.

But I am awake, sipping coffee,
warming my butt at the stove,
studying your watercolor of Acacia
as "Spiderman"—
a terrified child swinging through the void.

And Amber, now in her fourth month,
fist-sized, rocking in the amniotic fluid,
her face, like your paintings, unfinished
but taking form with each heartbeat
and the lightnings
that flicker across the umbilical.

I stare at your painting
and the terror in Acacia's face.
I think about all the sleeping faces,
and about Whitman's poem
on the dead Union soldiers,
their faces peaceful beneath the moonlight.

Oh at birth head and face push forward first
like a bowsprit into waves of light!

—*San Anselmo, 1980*

Sobaka in the Underworld

My cigar smells like a wet dog.
Outside night rain tars the street—
a glistening road to the underworld.
I put him to death
who loved me nine years;
who sat with me all day in the pickup
watching my face while I studied the bridge.

Dog-child and Man-dog,
I am dry-eyed in the Crisis Ward,
fearing my daughter's birth;
beaten with the metal leash of the Logos.
"Oh, master, I have served you
all my life."

We love dogs
because we have lost our bodies.
Logos split us.
No matter how often we copulate,
we are destined to wander,
looking for our hands and faces.

Earth, forgive me—
my guide through wet fields,
leaper and tearer at the beach—
I gave him a quick needle.

Dreamed him again last night,
old farter and itcher,
shaking off the dark river,
wondering where we might go next?

—*San Rafael, 1980*

Something Wakes You

Something wakes you.
The Dream
has you half-way eaten.
You flail around,
grope for the light switch.

You brush the antennae.
You try prying its jaws
from your hips.
You ache all over.
You are starting to lose fight.

With a hard twist
you manage to look
over your shoulder
at the Dream's fierce eyes
reflected in the estranged light
from the corner street lamp.

Outside a single car
goes by with its top
open to the summer night,
and two lovers laughing.
You think maybe
there is still time
to love; to be happy.

You make one last
thrust and torque,
but the Dream
has its teeth
in the base of your spine.

—*San Rafael, 1981*

Two From Rancho Cieneguilla

For James McGrath

Morning

The bird tracks in the dust
greet me as I jog down the road.
The green lichens and orange lichens
on the basalt ridge have awakened
and shoot out bands of light.
The petroglyphs make a clicking noise
as they brush their teeth.
In the orchard I hear the plums sweetening,
and the grass is ripe with pears and apples
that lie about like fallen drumbeats.

Hummingbird is up early, too,
blowing and sucking on the wildflowers
like Kokoapelli.
And oh, yes, Butterfly is not to be outdone—
she dances and leaps from sunflower to sunflower,
shaking out her black and orange silks.

Night

We have come here for dream time.
We have come to let the rock figures guide us.
We hear them whispering and singing in the dark.
Snake and Lightning watch over us.
Lizard, Frog and Beetle bless our sleep.
Holy Man raises his arms to the Sun Father,
whose black light shines on our sleeping faces.

We dream, we weep, we are overcome by the love
pouring down on us from the basalt ridge.
When we wake up we feel cleansed and healed.
We are filled with new power.
We come out of our tents to meet the day,
bearing new shields and lightning-tipped lances.

—*La Cieneguilla, 1981*

Drunk in Pecos

We smoked two joints and talked.
Then I drank too much wine
and she turned me out.
I learned again
what I had forgotten—
that she could be cold
as Pecos in winter.

But it was an August night
and I was sick-drunk.
I needed badly to screw and sing.
So her two dogs and I
climbed the rocks behind the house—
to dance, whirl, and howl
among deep juniper shadows.

Drunk in Pecos, New Mexico
on a summer night
I gave my lonely semen
to the full moon and the dust.

—*La Cieneguilla, 1981*

Written at Michael Good, Fine Books

In afternoon light, San Anselmo, California,
January 28th, 1982, the Year of the Dog.
Gross Morbid Anatomy of the Brain in the Insane
open on the desk, by I.W. Blackman, Pathologist
to the Government Hospital for the Insane,
Washington, D.C. 1908.

Blown magnolia tree at the window.
Pink flame of the tulip blossoms.
Plate XXVI, Autopsy No. 1969, Case 11960;
B.W.; aged 60; male, white; soldier; nativity,
Kentucky; mental disease, chronic epileptic dementia.
B.W.'s brain flayed open, showing effects
of hemorrhage, raw bleeding, gross morbid anatomy . . .

1982, the Year of the Dog, B.W., aged 46, nativity,
Missouri. Brain showing effects
of Gross Morbid Anatomy of U.S. culture;
wired on sugar, hooked into the flickering phantasms
of news and soaps: images of gratuitous violence.

1982. The Year of the Dogs.
Dogs wild in the streets. Plutonium in the rivers.
The decade of Book Burning
and why Johnny *won't* read.
Fantasy moguls filming in crypts,
hacks hacking, bleeding over their scripts.

Pink and white flames of the tulip blossoms.
Book husks heating the room.
The fire of words, breath and flame.
Bring us back to the body.
Brings us back to books.

Water Striders on Paper Mill Creek

After a lithograph by Richard Lang

Do they delight
in being lighter than water,
or is their only grace
that of predators?

Once I saw an emerald hopper
vault the creek and miss.
Oh, the water striders danced
then on their wet web,

came swiftly striding
on telegraph stilts
to cover the carapace
with living hair.

When they had finished
their gravy and meat
they picked their teeth,
told a few jokes

and then went dutifully back
to walking the surface tension
between fish and bird,
between shadow and sun.

—*Woodacre, 1983*

Irises

For Michael Good, bookseller & Sandra Good, bookbinder

Mike and Sandy
this is just to say
the dirt loves us.

Opened the kitchen curtain
for light
and was shaken awake
by your purple and yellow irises—
swollen and dripping color
on the morning canvas.

Iris, messenger from the gods
and goddess of the rainbow.
Beauty, dressed in her classic
and romantic robes,
or just pure flower, nameless.

And I, who have grown older
and more cynical
toward such invocation,
was already working another poem,
slurping a cup, and musing.

This is just to say
no matter how much in debt
or how miserably we primates
treat each other,
the earth loves us.

This morning I pulled
the curtain on your garden
and a rainbow
arced into my coffee cup.

—Woodacre, 1985

Amber & Acacia, Reagan & Gorbachev by Starlight

Acacia grouses
because she *hates* sleeping out.
"Cats will get us!
"Ants will crawl on us!"

And even outside,
drenched in nightly beauty,
Amber has her *clock* nightmare.

We four watch
the Kachina clouds go home,
leaving a vast, dark, crystal bowl.

The girls drift away to sleep.
A few stars, who want more light,
lean down to browse their blonde hair.

Stars, be kind to them
and to all sleeping children.
Let them live out their time.

Distill poetry and corrosive dew
in each and every missile silo.
Leak into the White House

and the Kremlin; secrete music
in Reagan's and Gorbachev's shoes—
that they might wake to a different dance.

—*San Anselmo, 1985*

ROOT HOG OR DIE

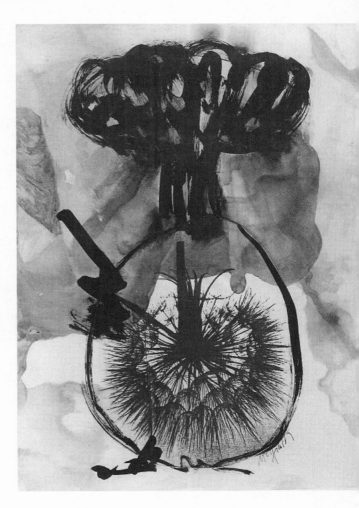

To Workman's Comp

For Bill Minor

I

When asked for last words before the noose
Francois Villon broke wind and said,
"Now my head will find out how much my ass weighs."
Hustling-ass myself in the feminine sounding
Town of Petaluma, I waltzed
Off the walkboard into air, my arms
Full of packing cartons.
It was not as grim as Villon's last day,
But I did find out how much my ass weighed
And the absolute inflexibility of asphalt.
This lumper took his lumps.

II

My problem here is where to end this:
The question of closure in poems written
In free verse and vernacular wit.
If you write in High Court
You might come to a rhetorical ending—
Unless you are one of those academic poets
Who has never roughened his paws with labor.
Then you can be clever, and drivel on.

III

I haven't gotten out of this;
Completely loaded the van.
If you wonder why I titled this
"To Workman's Comp," it's Econ I-A,
Learned on the job.
After a summer in the meat market
I cashed out my own beef.
220 lbs of aged male poet
Paid $640.00 accident insurance.

IV

This manifest
Comes to you courtesy
Of Transprotection Service Company,
St. Louis, Missouri,
And by way of United Van Lines,
Larkspur, California.
Thus ends my tale
Of how much my tail is worth.

—*Larkspur-Petaluma, 1983*

My Father Dying: 1984

He hums with prostate cancer.
Carried plutonium home in his underwear,
Ashes of Trinity, ashes of Nagasaki.

"For Christ's sake, dad,
You went to work daily out of love
And duty, but did the Devil's job.
You guys stoked Hell's ovens,
Brought home shadows in your lunchboxes.

"All the discarded radiation badges
Did not monitor how much your children love you,
Or measure thirty years of labor
Smoldering in your work pants;
Or count the sperm spitting across centuries,
Igniting everywhere karmaic fires."

—*Richland*

Once by Hanford Reach

I cupped an exploded milkweed pod—
The air so still
Seeds would not shake out;
The light in the husk
Both blinding and delicate—
Like that moment at Ground Zero
When eye pods implode
Dark seeds of death-light.

—*Richland, 1985*

Nuke City Ballad

My home is Rattlesnake Mountain,
I'm bald as a river goose.
Me and my pal, Coyote,
Live on wind and yellowcake snoose.

> *Sing ki-yi yippi*
> *And doo-dah, doo-dah,*
> *I'm a Nuke City Boy!*

Oh, we went down to Nuke City
To get drunk and kick some ass;
To grab us a little titty
And piss on the gov'ment grass.

> *Sing ki-yi yippi*
> *And doo-dah, doo-dah,*
> *I'm a Nuke City Boy!*

We bust into Uptown Tavern,
We bellied up to the bar.
When the barmaid refused Coyote,
He showed off his keloid scar.

> *Sing ki-yi yippi*
> *And doo-dah, doo-dah,*
> *I'm a Nuke City Boy!*

Some Hanford boys was there,
They stood us a chain of beers.
They'd never seen such a wonderful scar
In all their forty years.

> *Sing ki-yi yippi*
> *And doo-dah, doo-dah,*
> *I'm a Nuke City Boy!*

Coyote got drunk 'n horny,
Started nipping the bar maid's jeans.
"I don't sleep with dogs," she said,
And radioed in the Marines.

> *Sing ki-yi yippi*
> *And doo-dah, doo-dah,*
> *I'm a Nuke City Boy!*

We had us quite a fracas,
We had us quite a brawl.
We left the Marines and the Hanford Boys
A-bleeding, one and all.

> *Sing ki-yi yippi*
> *And doo-dah, doo-dah,*
> *I'm a Nuke City Boy!*

Our home is Rattlesnake Mountain,
Our greens is Russian thistle.
We get our salt at the Hanford Lick,
And our meat is human gristle.

> *Sing ki-yi yippi*
> *And doo-dah, doo dah,*
> *I'm a Nuke City Boy!*

—*Richland, 1986*

A Rufous: Tomales, 1986

A Rufous
Mad about the fuschias
Darts and sucks noisily
His soup of nectar and gnats.

I stop shaking
My typewriter castanet
And watch—
His flickering gorget
Has set the bush on fire.

This
Is what we are born for
And from,
A nectar of sperm and flame.

Yet over the Pacific
An SR71 Blackbird
Shatters the air.
Glowing titanium, crimson.

Needle nosed,
Dipping and buzzing,
Its gorget threatens us
With blossoms of nuclear fire.

Working Class Haiku

Scorpion shadow
of the backhoe falls
on a ditch deep as my grave.

Coda:

I was tripping out on the feathery
patterns I was making in the sand
with my square edge shovel when
the super appeared at the ditch
bank and said, "Jesus Christ, Witherup,
we're not making a work of art here!
Hurry it up, man!"

—*Union laborer construction job,*
San Rafael, 1984

Portrait of S. B., with a Steel Wing

I

Sterling wears a steel wing,
A pipe organ of struts and screws
Riveting the bones of his *left* arm.

He is both Buddha
And wounded falcon
Is this shaman and falconer.

He rests his arm
On two pillows while we talk.
The irony

Is that I have come
For therapy about a trauma
To my *right* arm.

We enjoy
The humor of the situation—
Both of us savaged

On the plane
Of the Third World:
Sterling by a swerving

Panel truck crammed with
His client by a berserk
South Vietnamese Brevt. Maj.

II

On the matter of the hatchet
Attack by Maj. Thong Van Ho,
Sterling advises,

"When eating dinner
With a fiend,
Use a long spoon!"

We roar
And belly laugh
Until our wounded arms throb.

My insight *back*
Is that his arm was nearly sliced off
By a rearview-mirror!

We hoot and whuff again—
(We have a thoroughly
Good time together.)

III

As I leave the session,
Sterling salutes me
With his fractured wing,

And I waft into the air currents
Unhooded, sharper,
Ecstatic in the ultra-violet clouds!

—Berkeley, 1986

Egret: Bolinas Lagoon, 1986

Morning. Soap-shaving of a moon.
Sky and lagoon nacreous.
Sr. Ortega y Gasset
Stands reed-still
Examining the muck and weeds
For a metaphysical flash—
The meat of things.

Feathered white snake,
The Beautiful incarnate.
Head poised like a javelin.
Or hunched back on his feathers
Like a scholar
Studying an ancient text.

Even when he stalks
He does not move;
Turns the pages of water
Imperceptibly

While around him
His noisy students, the gulls,
Who have watched too much T.V.
And gobbled excessive junk food,
Cannot sit still, or concentrate.

They thwack and yawp around his desk,
Complaining about difficult homework.
They do not understand poetry
Or philosophy. They threaten
To tell their parents
And the School Board
That Professor Egret
Is a martinet.

He closes the lesson
With a firm and irritable croak,
And slams the door.
His exit is a marginal note
On Aesthetics and The Real.

Disciplined, economic,
Proving less is more,
He gathers the sky and moon
In his monkish sleeves
And makes of his leave-taking
A metaphor.

from the Bed and Breakfast Basement

At ground level
Peonies and white lilac
Imagine they are clouds.
Holsteins fatten on the April grasses,
Grow rounder and more feminine
Than the Marin hills.

The old guest house
Strains at its hawser,
Wanting to plunge off to the west,
Into the great waves of crimson light.

All the guests
Have rowed back to town
And to work. They slept late.
They made love;
Promised they would be back.

Below deck the First Mate
Sits on his bunk
Smoking English Ovals,
Badly wanting a drink.
He and the coffee pot
Are empty, exhausted, chuffed out.

His cabin is damp—
March storms battered the porthole,
And a school of sow bugs poured in.
They wax on the rotting woodwork,
On the flaking paint—
Like Exxon oil executives.

Earwigs, pillbugs, millipedes
Swarm on the First Mate's pillow;
Copulate in his boots.
The cabin blackens with them—
Until the house goes down,

Sucking behind it cows, barns,
Sheep and a pregnant stray cat
Waiting outside
For a bowl of milk.

—Tomales, 1987

Root Hog or Die

Well, I went to California in the year of Seventy-six,
When I landed there, I was in a turrible fix,
Didn't have no money vittles for to buy
And the only thing for me was to—Root hog or die!
                    —American Folk Song

I'm no craftsman in wood
Or stone masonry.
I'm always the laborer
Or carpenter's helper.

But I've learned this much—
I can snap a line.
A chalk marker, perfectly plucked,
Will leave on stud, sheetrock
Or stone a horizon
Of blue dust.

But today, and last month,
I'm out of work—
There's no call now
For Line-Snappers.

So buddy, or lady,
If you're taking up the trade
Let me give you some advice—
It's—*Root hog or die!*

—Petaluma, 1987

Variations on an Image by W. C. Williams

I

So much depends
Upon

An orange Clark
Forklift

Crusted with calcium
Nitrate

Beside three tons
Of *Turf Surpreme*

II

Red orange
Mast

Greasy chain
A nearly

Sexual pleasure
Depends upon

Slipping forks
Pefectly into the keys

III

Thrusting steel
Blades

Into the earth's
Guts

So much profit
And power

Depends upon the North
Americans' love for *Techne*

IV

So much
Profit

Excessive and
Particular

Profit; forks
Disembowel

Particular countries;
Men and women with names

V

Particular names
Chevron

Dow, Dupont
Dumping

Unsafe pesticides
On the Guatemalan

Market for instance
So much profit

VI

Depends upon
A laborer

In Honduras
Say

Spraying a fungicide
In the greenhouse

No gloves, no mask
Death his profit

VII

Soldiers in dustmasks
Raise

The dead on
Biers

Fork the pallets
Of body bags

Three tons
Of *Turf Supreme*

VIII

"Take your profit
And shove it!"

My work gloves are
Stained

With more than
Nitrates—

My Honduran brother's
Scarred, milky corneas

—*Petaluma, 1987*

Chama

Eros and Logos were one to her:
A passion for truth in men.
Her love bites grated on bone.

She left me for love of Nietzsche:
Found men merely mortal;
Went through us all

Like fire in dry chaparral.
An ember smoldered in her womb,
Fed by sexual oils—

Blazed out in the toss
Of her hair. There was
Conflagration everywhere.

Nor am I done with her:
She waits for me
At the top of the stair

Her fevers
Metastasized into the tumor
Of 8,000 hungers.

—Tomales, 1988

Mervyn Clyde Witherup

b. July 14, 1910—d. May 12, 1988

Nearing the end
Father was all bones and pain.
The tumor had eaten him
Down to the rind.

Yet little he complained
Or whined. Sulfate of morphine
Eased him somewhat and he kept
His mind and wit—

Though talking was difficult.
A dry wind off the volcanic desert
Went through each of his rooms
Snuffing out cells;

Left and alkaloid crust
On his tongue. We stood by
With Sponge-On-A-Stick
When he was assaulted by thirst

And images. "Give me your hand,"
He said. "And lead me to
The water cooler. I've been
Up in the sky—I'm very tired."

Then, irritated with us,
He would ask to be left alone.
He would suck a sponge and grab
The lifting bar; be off again

Brachiating from cloud to cloud.
"Is there a station near by?
How do we get out of here?
You'll have to help me, son."

He died on graveyard shift.
The train came for him at 3 A.M.,
And when he ran to catch it,
He was out of breath.

—Richland, 1988

Sir, if You Are, Sir

Sir, if you are, sir—the unnameable flame,
Forgive this lapsed Methodist
His present trade: his tackle, gear
And trim; the company truck—
Twelve floot flatbed International
With which he purveys and delivers
Chemical fertilizers and such pesticides
As *Roundup, Ronstar, Surflan, Baygon,*
Metaldehyde, Trimec, Dymec, Gopher Bait,
2,4,D and *Mole Blasters—all to blight*
And sear the dearest freshness
Deep down things; that the wealthy
Might golf on jeweled turf, or Man Suburban
Contemplate a weedless lawn.

Man's smell, man's smudge are everywhere:
The soil is bare and we
Have torn a hole in the very sky.
Some nestlings are born blind now—
Yet we ignore the evidence.
Getting and spending, we lay waste.

Sir, if you are, sir—your supplicant
Wishes he could work for you daily;
Might walk naked the wild meadows—
Be wafted on flower-light and wind
Up, up, up, raptor-like, rapturously.
Yet he is tied down as he ties down
His load, and valued for his trucker's hitch—
The craft of ropes; not for the craft
Of naming and divining the unnameable flame.

—Petaluma, 1988

Gathering Blackberries

I wish I could spend three days grieving:
Hiroshima/Nagasaki—fingers purple-stained,
Wrists raw from thorns. How easily
Ripe ones pull off—skin, testicles, nipples—
The largest nearly the size of a baby's eye.
Suddenly we go from blossom to berry to seed.
Dear Christ, Dear Buddha I offer
One blackberry for each thousand A-bomb deaths.

—*Forestville, August 6, 1988*

Our President Reads a Book— Not Louis L'Amour

Before all the world
Our president kneels on the White House
Lawn; silences his helicopter blades
Alerted to take Ronald Reagan to his wife.

Ronald gestures with his hand
To halt the Secret Service—
Who are alarmed to see the boss
What?—gut-shot, committing *sepuku*?

Now our President takes a book
From his trench coat, reads aloud.
That book is Whitman; it is Rilke;
It is Gabriela Mistral—we are amazed!

As he begins he chokes up.
He weeps for Nancy Reagan's mastectomy;
Cries for all the women
Under his Administration.

Also, "it seems" children
In Lebanon, Iran, inner Des Moines
Have had legs and arms sliced off
By words from North America.

Then Ronald Reagan stands tall,
Wipes his nose on his sleeve
And his voice turns over, throbs, hums,
Flattens the grass—lines from Akhmatova,

Neruda beat above us like rotor blades.
We are relieved, we are glad,
Ronald Reagan has become human in public.
We have sought his love for a thousand days.

—*Forestville, 1988*

Charlie Parker, 1989

Art is labor; art is rage.
You think Charlie Parker
Was just some "stoned nigger"
Who blew toot toot? Have you watched
A man hunt?—Charlie could
Outrun any Afrikaaner's whippet.

Our Afrikaaners touch the brims
Of their black hats, say Thee and Thou;
Think they have God's right
To work any "red nigger" to death.

Charlie was in pain. Those black hats
Slice everybody up. Charlie hurt,
But he went to work. He left dust
On their buckle shoes. He ran
That buffalo down—buried his face
In its belly and fed on hot, steaming sound.

Art is hard. You need a tough heart
And good wind. You hyenas hang back.
Let the lion eat. You'll have your chance
At gobbets. You can whine and fawn then;
Scoot your butts in the dirt.

—*Petaluma*

The Coming of Desire

Satan was a mustard eye on a green field.
His hammered scales were rusted
After long, hard duty at the Logos Tree;
His bowels acid with the ration
Of burnished apples; Satan craved red meat!

A violet light shone in the rushes.
A smell neither floral nor arboreal
Grabbed Satan's tongue and mustard eye.
And just about snapped them out of his skull.
His copper-green tail twitched DANGER.

An animal Satan had not yet seen
Walked out of the reeds.
It had a long mane that flickered
With blue lightnings, like a thunderhead.
Satan radioed, "Logos to Patriarchy!"

Patriarchy sent forth all its power
While centurion Satan laid low,
Jerked with spasms. Adrenalin fanned
Along his scales—he went rigid.
The Logos Tree shuddered, spat fire.

It was a battle of light. The Tree
Crackled silver, vermillion.
Lt. Satan rose to strike, dripping
Mercury, uranium. But the animal came on,
Fearlessly: spread its feet in the mud

Until Satan saw a radiance; his tongue
Sensed a heat that was not found
Previously on earth. He knew it was over;
He would resign his commission; lay his flat head
In that animal's belly; hole up there forever.

—*Tigris/Euphrates River deltas, 5000 BC*

DOWN WIND, DOWN RIVER

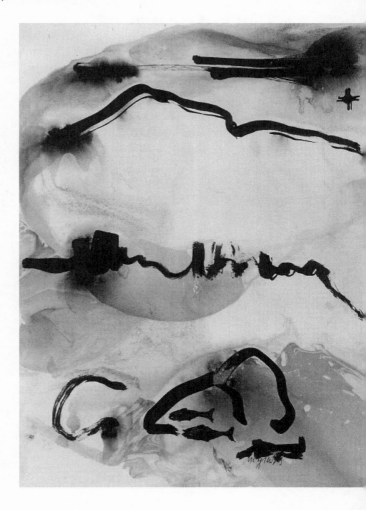

Not-So-Still-Life

White cherry blossoms
Float the Quad.
Froth of petals and light.
Wave-green the grass.

A crow in the mast
Of the Art Building
Keeps a sharp eye out for jetsam—
Pieces of sandwich, Karmelkorn.

In a voice that is
The fast shake of a dice cup,
Our Lookout calls down
Caustic advice to lovers.

At dusk the corby flaps
Over to his bachelor nest
In Music, where his sleep
Is broken by the chords

Of desire; where he dreams
About taking her in a tree,
Blossoms on her back and tail;
Her biting smell in his beak.

—*Seattle, 1990*

Snow White

She was beautiful, lying there in the meadow,
Pretending sleep.
When I leaned over to kiss her forehead
She placed my hand on her breast.
Her nipples swelled and stirred.
As I peeled back the counterpane
Her pussy ignited.
I fled into the fir grove,
My shirt on fire.

When the sheriff and her forester-husband
Came to arrest me for arson,
I was on my knees, lapping Snow White
Like a dog. She had not told me
She had a wedding ring beneath her pillow.
The judge nailed me for adultery—
I could not deny the evidence;
Had third degree burns on my face and chest.

The prison doc put ointment on the burns.
I am due for a skin graft.
I am planning an escape,
Though I know the hounds will track me
Into the farthest and darkest bush.
Because I have Snow White
All over me—can not scrub off her smell—
Even with this gritty, brown, slammer soap.

—*Seattle, 1991*

Coda

Docs have released the poet
From the Psych Ward
After weeks of chemical lobotomies.
Music up, and soft gels
On his beloved, waiting in the corridor,
With arms outstretched.
"I love and respect you," says she
In her best blow-job voice.

He staggers past—a man
Still with a chest full of hornets;
Turns on his heel, Bogart-like,
And says, "I was a chump
To think the Muse would be faithful!
Did not know you were the town whore.
Now that I have popped those cherries,
Kiddo, see ya around the literary neighborhood.
And stay wet!"

—Seattle, 1991

At the Poetry Furnace

At the immense furnace shoveling coke
With a big snow scoop.
Asbestos gloves, steel-toed boots;
Stripped to the belt, goggles
To keep corneas from melting.
My father died here, at Furnace 3—
Thirty years toe-to-toe with the fire,
Vermillion chevrons on his torso.

Some females tried it, E.E.O.
Oh it was good for the blood
Sweating and levering beside
Bare-titted women!—
But Human Resources sent the girls
Over to Moon and Mystery;
Declared this roiling heat a man's job.

Driving home after a twelve hour shift,
Aching in every muscle and pore,
I pop a cold Bud, put Bach on the tape deck
And wheel my pickup home
Through the great star-borne radio tides.

—*1993, Milky Way, the Cosmos*

Motorcycle Moon

For Tatiana Schwemmer, in Chelyabinsk

The motorcycle moon, on night dispatch,
Exhausted, acid-mouthed, low on petrol;
Bears messages for Mayakovsky, Yesenin—
Stalin orders, "You poets go to hell."

The suicidal moon, disgusted with itself,
Flings off goggles and gloves,
Kills the motor; kneels at the Techa River
And drinks hungrily of yttrium and ferro cyanide.

The proverbial rooster can not clear his throat;
Sends the barnyard bitch to find the dawn.
She fetches back a ticking piece of jawbone
To feed her pups. "Here, Comrade," she barks,
"Our friend the moon has broken its neck."

—Seattle, 1993

John Wayne, Gunslinger, R.I.P.

John Wayne, gunslinger, pranced out
From the White City on the Hill.
At White Bluffs—"Way out West, podner!"—
Alpha, Beta and Gamma
Charged back and forth,
Whooping it up, having a great time—
Cayuses hoofing chalky dust.
The braves mooned John; pissed
Off the cliff; waggled their dicks at him.
"We have your wives! We have your sons.
What you going do, whitey?"
Wayne was cool, unflinching—
A face one wears before Big Evil.
The moment his gelding's forlegs
Splashed into the icy, fast flowing river,
A pitchy-tumored arrow thunked
Smack in the wet brain
Of our hero-gunslinger, John Wayne.

—*Seattle, 1993*

Late Spring, after the Gulf War

Cesium drips from the horse chestnut trees.
Bush has Graves Disease (and a fear of death).
Huge, gorgeous, pink and red poppies
Collapse like gassed lungs.
Each leaf and blossom
Is infected with Republican lies.

—*Seattle, 1993*

Nagasaki Journal: August 9, 1945

The light coughed;
Cleared its throat of matter;
Spat a tarry ball of hot mucous
On *Homo sapiens sapiens.*

Buddha wept; then laughed.
He spun a Water Lilly—
Flashing signals throughout
The Milky Way and Andromeda

That Birth and Death
Were temporarily arrested
And that souls
Simmering in the vaginal

Petri dishes on planet earth
Would have to take a new number
And wait in line
For another fifty years.

—Seattle, 1993

Living by I-5, August 6, 1995

No, not the 100,000 year-old ice dam
At Lake Missoula bursting—flooding
Scablands at Hanford and Wallula Gap.
Not diastole or systole of the Pacific
Sucking sand and gravel—but roaring,
Licking Hell-flame.

Started up
From a drugged, Trazadone sleep—
Cave where I was hiding; a tank spat
Burning jelly, coating me with Truman
Postage stamps, hot scabs I could not peel.

Woke up to "Yes, that freeway susuration
Is Hell-flame"; cars and trucks hurtling by
Are ghosts of Hiroshima and Nagasaki dead
Yet fleeing that quick lick of white fire.
Melted faces looking for a lost eye,
A missing breast—

Souls tortured as any at Auschwitz,
Belsen, Dachau flayed for lampshades—
These dead are burning headlights at 2:00 am.
And there are demons on the overpasses
In labcoats and dark goggles, checking
Dosimeters for permissible radiation levels.

At dawning the sun explodes—
An orange flash shakes my windows.
Swallows, after the first stir and seethe
Of insects, ignite in air.
There is a terrible stench from the freeway—
Each car has an aura of blue flame.

—*Seattle*

My Grandson at Green Lake

Shane Gabriel Diamond, just two,
Feeds bread to the ducks and gulls.
November sun takes his blond hair.
The green sheen on the drakes' necks
Echoes the park grass where maple, oak
And plum have dropped a yellow and rose
Tapestry of leaves. The crabapple trees
Are bare but for thick, whirling
Dark-red constellations of fruit.

The boy has a devilish laugh.
He has come to earth to enjoy himself.
When a greedy mallard nips his finger
Shane holds it up for *g'ampa* to kiss it.
This gesture summons radiance
To crackle across the lake and roil
Around him—he is both Gabriel
And Demeter, bringing bread and light.

—*Seattle, 1995*

Still (Active) Life with Plum Tree, Man, and Dog

Unlike some of my fellow primates
The plum tree is generous.
It is not running for office
Or trying to profit from its looks.

It stretches; seems to strain
Branches upward and outward.
Were it not rooted, might walk
Over and embrace us.

Though Nonseq and I are not certain
What map to follow the rest of our
Journey on earth, we take a risk;
Wade into the tall grasses.

The sweet-smelling torches
Of the plum tree branches
Light the way, blossoms dropping
Before us like flaming embers.

—*Seattle, 1996*

Walking Nonseq in New Snow

In the Beginning were deuterium,
Helium, and hydrogen—
The universe was compressed
Into a fistful of light.

Non Sequitur leaps ahead
In the newly fallen snow.
We are the first outside—
Primate and canid.
A flake of moon flashlights the field.

There is so much to say
About the joy squeezed
Into the basic nouns *dog* and *snow;*
And our two hearts pumping in tandem
As we leave paw-prints—
Wells of dark light.

My dog and I were there
At the Big Bang. So were you.
Let us remember we myriad life forms
Began our journey as a palmful of fire;
And let us be kind and love one another
As we fling into the year 2000.

—Seattle, 1996

For Mumia Abu-Jamal, on Pennsylvania's Death Row

Panting underneath the rhododendrons
With his hoard of lime-green tennis balls
He won't fetch back, my Corgie-Labrador
Lies inside a house of light.

Clouds flow by, flicking the swollen
Pink-white bushes on an off.
I send you this word-bouquet, Mumia,
And the images of a dog at play

In exhange for the brightness of your courage
And the filaments of intelligence that flash
From the pages of *Live From Death Row*.

II

"Wing guard, I'm calling Mumia Abu-Jamal
Long distance on the sepal-phone.
And I have a message for you and the other
Guards in SCI Green County:

The light in the rhododendron flower
Will be the lightning in the barbed wire.
The heat of Mumia's thought
Will burn the blindfold from Justice.

The *word* is more powerful than your
Handguns and bullying batons.
Turn in your weapons; open the cells;
Embrace the prisoners as your brothers.

History, the laborers, the peasants,
The poor and the underclasses
Are weary of being starved and murdered.
The radiance in the rhododendrons

Is the light of love, of brotherhood
And sisterhood. Let the men and women
Out in the yard. Tell the warden, 'We quit.'
Tell him the voices of poets present

And poets past, who have been imprisoned
Or silenced for speaking truth, are on
The flower telephones, and that we
Are jamming the lines in Mumia's behalf."

—*Seattle, 1996*

Two for Sophie Dog

1

For painter/poet Alan Chong Lau

It was an ink on rice paper day;
Dollops of snow broken by raw, sharp
Angles of deadfall branches.
My sister's Lab, Sophie, rolled in mud,
Vying with the crows for deepest black.

—*Seattle, 1993*

2

For my sister, Sandra Hankins

We returned from cancer's kingdom
And a gathering of the clan
To find that her hip tumor
Was humming like a Hanford tank.

Sandra held panther-headed Sophie
While the vet administered
A jolt of phenobarbitol.
Put away her feeding bowl.

At Richland's Tower Inn
I had a waking, fitful dream
That all the souls who died
From labor at the weapons plant

Were dragonflies flitting above
The waste tanks, as if those poison silos
Were a demonic form of water lily.
There were dog-souls out there,

Jim – neglected to enclose the errata

errata **Down Wind, Down River, William Witherup, West End Press:**

p 49 line 11: "back and forth *over*
the River Road"

p 50 line 9: "I *see* him as he truly is"

p 102 line 19: "Panel truck crammed with *campesinos*"

p 135 line 19: "Death, who recycles all *biota*"

Beagles that gave their lives
For National Security—injected
With plutonium, fed Tritium-laced milk;
Had bones broken for medical science.

Put away their feeding bowls.
Panther-headed Sophie joins them
In the galaxy reserved for wolves,
Coyotes, foxes and dogs.

A Labrador would eat all the time
If she had the opportunity.
But a cancer cell never gets its fill.
Put away Sophie's feeding bowl,

Who dished out nine years of pure dog love,
A food some primates need to live.
Ravenna creek will miss her paws;
Her muzzle dipping for a drink.

When we walk Cowen Park now
The creek sounds will trigger grief.
Death, who recycles all biotad,
Has lapped up Sophie dog.

—Richland-Seattle, 1997

Salmon Speaks

Grandmother and grandfather swam
The humming river before it was befouled
With pesticides and bleaches, its soul
Broken by dams, turbines, dredges.

The old stories were fishtailed in sand,
In pictures on canyon walls.
We knew the joy of fresh water
Roaring past our gills.

We taught First People courage—
How to take flow and force head on.
We showed them honor; we sang
Our death songs in spawning pools.

Our brilliant eggs mothered clans
And words. From round fish mouth
Came the sounds *moon* and *drum*.
Leaping through the taut skin

Of pools we saw stars flash
In our scales; fish eye mirrored
The core of the Hourglass Nebula,
And otoliths the navigation of light.

—*Seattle, 1997*

The Baker of Pies

This trip Rose bakes pumpkin pies;
She is never so happy as when transmuting
Dough and sugar. How many cherry, peach,
Pumpkin and apple pastries have fissioned
From her eighty-three-year-old fingers?

Last August it was deep-dish blueberry
Made for her elder son.
But the pie leapt from its dish,
Nearly scalding her leg; left
A purple double-helix on the carpet.

Today I am raking leaves; carrying on
Conversation with the sycamores.
They signal they can smell the spice,
Sugar and pumpkin working their alchemies.

Thirty miles northeast from the family duplex
Hanford tank-sludge cooks and shifts
From stable to unstable—the ticking nucleides
Not musical, unlike the drum-brushing branches.

AEC/DOE might have put mother
In charge of a tank farm.
No crust would have been unpinched;
No detail overlooked; no graft or lies.

Inside the house a mild November
Afternoon, an old woman with a nose
For chemistry has her hand on the controls;
Sniffs the wind and watches the boilers
As we sail out of the Twentieth Century.

—*Richland, 1998*

When the Computers Have Crashed

When the computers have crashed
And Finance Capital exhausted
Its supply of fresh blood,
There will yet be the scent
Of sagebrush on the wind,
And the flicker of a full moon
In a coyote's eye.

The Suits might get in touch
With their emotions then.
They will pound their chests,
Grief-stricken; ask themselves
Why they did not read the poets?

Some will wander the scablands
Near the abandoned Hanford reactors;
Whistle for their feral dogs
That have joined coyote packs;
Apologize to the jackrabbits
And the lovely, beating grouse.

The Suits might fling out their arms
Then to the rushing-away constellations,
And be unashamed of the tears
Glistening on their faces
And beading their lips.

—*Seattle, 1998*

The Scientific-Technological Paradigm

After an image by Frank Waters

"After the first A-bomb test,"
The rancher said,
Some of my horses went blind.
When they stumbled and rolled over
Their manes and backs had gone white."

The nuclear-bomb-and-missile-guys
Hate life itself. They will jab
A contaminated stick
In Pegasus' eye and call it *data*.
Then they will cut off one wing
To wipe their asses with
After a shit and a coffee break.

—*Seattle, 1999*

Down Wind, Down River

For Frederick Wayne Nelson, down river,
who was in the bio-path of the Green Run, 1949

Oh say can you breathe
By the dawn's early wind
What so proudly we made
At Hanford Engineering Works:
Iodine-131, plutonium, ruthenium.

At the dawn's early light
Irradiated meadowlarks
Filled a young boy's heart
With isotopes of beauty.
Particle and wave shimmered
Over the river stones.

What so proudly we hailed.
Looking for arrowheads
After my morning paper route,
By the hot Columbia;
Bike sparkling with flakes
Of mica not mica.

"Roll on Columbia," Woody.
Salmon smolt stunned
As they hit the outflow plumes.
At twilight's last gleaming
I-131 sifting on sage and thistle,
On sweet, newly-cut alfalfa.

Plutonium in the hog swill,
Ruthenium in the jackrabbit's eye.
The pure products of America go crazy.
By the dawn's early light
Hiroshima flickers white-hot,
Nagasaki fuses with the sun.

Particle and wave,
What physicists proudly hailed,
Who used murderous intellect
To invent deadly winds; military
And scientific elite gassing their own
Workers, soldiers, and children.

Down river, down wind;
I-131, plutonium, ruthenium.

—*Seattle, 1996*

Envoi: Manic Depression in the Rear-View Mirror

The highway snaps and flaps behind me:

See Bill in Big Sur, about to quaff
A cup of hemlock. It smells like mouse piss.
He starts to gag. His lover
Knocks it from his hand.

And there is Bill again, at the railing
Of the Golden Gate Bridge.
His eyes are already dead.
You could drop steel ballbearings
In his eye sockets and they would
Never hit bottom.

Because he has daughters
And a newborn, Bill signals
The State Patrol. On the way
To the nut house the officer
Tells Bill about his own divorce
And his partner in LA who fingerprinted
His brains on the wall—over a woman.

See Bill in the loony bin.
He is in a foetal position
And sucking his thumb. He knows
This is not a manly thing to do.
The psychiatric nurse, also male,
Tells him that he will get over it.
He, the nurse, once slit his wrists
Over a failed love affair.
Why he became a psychiatric nurse—
One of the most miserable of callings.

Bill's publisher asks him
On the drive from Santa Fe
To the Albuquerque airport,
"Why don't you write a memoir—
You've led such an interesting life?"
Bill glances in the rear view mirror.
He sees Beauty skipping into the sagebrush.

She is bare-ass naked; hasn't aged a whit.
Her titties are still firm, perky
And pink nippled.
"John," he said. "I can't write a memoir
Because I haven't caught Beauty yet.
To grab that woman, you have to kick it
Into manic gear; now I'm sixty-four,
I have an arthritic knee,

And Beauty is a Shape Shifter—
When you are just about to grip
Her inner thigh,
And you are out of breath
You find you have fallen
Into a nest of rattlesnakes."

—*La Cieneguilla-Seattle, 1999*

I GO DREAMING ROADS

Translations

Antonio Machado
Vicente Huidobro
Enrique Lihn
Olzhas Suleimenov

Some Notes on Translation

Somewhere in my notebooks I have a quote from Paul Valery that the very process of writing poetry is one of translation. Poets translate from the language of everyday speech. When you translate a poet from another language and culture into your own native tongue, the process gets even more complex. And when you work with co-translators, as I have done here, you have two separate languages and three voices. It is a process that begins to sound like the founding of the Catholic Church! What did Jesus really say in Aramaic? And when did he say it?

It is an old saw, but I whang it again: You can't translate poetry. You can translate the imagery and metaphor, but you lose the sound-image, which is also part of the original meaning of the poem. Though English is a language rich in both vowels and consonants, no matter how much you monkey with a Spanish poem the English version loses the sonority and rhythm of the original Spanish, a language ripe with vowels and feminine endings. And when you lose the sound-image, you may also lose the nuances of tone. What you end up with is an approximation.

And the poem in English will also take on the voice of the translator. Machado, Huidobro, and Lihn come to you here in my voice. Both Serge Echeverria, a native Chilean who has lived in San Francisco for many years, and Carmen Scholis, a former teacher of Spanish in the Monterey, California public schools, did the hardest job of it, the first versions; I worked from their trots, so to speak. At the time, I read enough Spanish to be able to get a feel for the poem in the native tongue. And Serge and Carmen would also read the originals aloud.

Carmen and I came to translate Machado after we were looking at an anthology of contemporary Spanish poetry by Ben Bellitt. Carmen was incensed at Bellitt's translation of Machado's "En memoria de Abel Martín" and I suggested, hey, why don't we play around with some Machado versions of our own, and we did. Our main purpose was to send the little volume out for Christmas presents, which we did, but we also sold quite a few to university libraries. It was published by Peters Gate Press in Monterey, in an edition of 250 copies.

Serge and I worked on Vicente Huidobro, who wrote both in Spanish and French, because he was one of Serge's favorite poets. In fact, if one believed in reincarnation or karma, I would risk saying that Serge Echeverria and Vicente Huidobro are the same person. Ward Abbott, editor of *Desert Review* which was then in Santa Fe, brought out our co-translation of *Arctic Poems* in an edition of 500 copies.

It was Robert Bly who suggested that I try my hand at translating Enrique Lihn. His voice ranged from the intense nature lyric through poems of social and political content, to intricate, sometimes bitter verses about love, marriage, and family. Sometimes he mixes and compresses these various voices in the same poem. Lihn's syntax could be quite quirky and vernacular, but Serge piloted us through the coral reefs. The late William Matthews along with Russell Banks, who at the time co-edited *Lillabulero* magazine, brought out *This Endless Malice* in an edition of 500 copies.

The final poem in this set of translations comes from another source. The author, Olzhas Suleimenov, a geologist from Kazakhstan, was in the Soviet Duma before the fall of the Berlin Wall and was instrumental in putting a stop to nuclear testing in his republic. The reader can decide whether his poem about a blind man he saw in the Louvre is political or not.

—William Witherup
  March-July, 2000

Biographies of Co-translators

SERGE ECHEVERRIA: Chilean born; world traveler, stage actor, language instructor, and translator, tour lecturer, court interpreter. Lived in Europe. Resides in San Francisco.

CARMEN OLAETA SCHOLIS: A graduate of the Monterey Institute of International Studies, she has studied and traveled in Spain and South America. She taught high school Spanish for thirty years in the Monterey Public School System and continues to teach Spanish to adults.

Antonio Machado

Antonio Machado (1875–1939) was born in the Andalusian city of Seville. After studying at the University of Madrid and the Sorbonne in Paris, he returned to Spain in 1912. He died in exile in the French Pyrennes near the end of the Spanish Civil War. His poetry is intimate; the reflections of a solitary man on his environment, the landscapes of Andalusia and especially of Castille. In his love of the Spanish people, he aligns himself with the Generation of '98, exploring traditional meters of the Spanish popular ballads and romances.

Yo voy soñando caminos

I Go Dreaming Roads

I go dreaming roads
of the afternoon. The golden
hills, the green pines,
the dusty oaks! . . .
Where will the road go?
I go singing, traveler
along the footpath . . .
the afternoon is falling.
"I had the thorn of passion
in my heart;
I managed to pull it out one day:
I no longer feel my heart."

And the whole field remains
a moment, dark and mute,
meditating. The wind sounds
in the poplars by the river.

The afternoon grows darker;
and the winding road
turns faintly white,
grows obscure and vanishes.

My singing returns to lamenting:
"Sharp golden thorn,
who could feel you
nailed in his heart."

Cante Hondo

I was meditating, absorbed, winding
the threads of boredom and sadness,
when I heard
through the window of my room, open

to a warm summer night,
the wailing of a lazy ballad,
broken by the somber tremolos
of my land's magical musicians.

. . . And it was Love, like a red flame . . .
a nervous hand put a long golden sigh
on the vibrating string,
which was changed to a fountain of stars—

. . . And it was Death, the knife in the shoulder,
the long pass, grim and skeletal.
So I dreamed it when I was a child—

And on the guitar, resonant and trembling,
the brusque hand, striking, mimicked
the blow of a coffin on the earth.

And it was a lonely weeping, a breath
the dust sweeps away and the ash expels.

A Youthful Figure Comes

A youthful figure comes
to our place one day.
We ask her: "Why do you return
to the old house?"
She opens the window, and the whole countryside
of light and smell drifts in.
On the white path
the tree trunks are turning black;
the topmost leaves
are green smoke dreaming in the distance.
The broad river
seems like a lagoon in the white
morning haze. Through the violet mountains
another chimera is walking.

Campo
Field

The afternoon is dying
like a lowly hearth burning out.

There on the mountains
a few embers remain.

And that broken tree on the white road
makes you weep for pity.

Two branches on the wounded trunk, and one
stained black leaf on each branch!

Are you crying? . . . Between the golden poplars,
in the distance, love's darkness waits for you.

Canciones de tierras altas

Songs from the Highlands

I

Through the white mountains . . .
the light snow
and the wind in your face.

Among the pines . . .
the road being erased
by white snow.

Strong wind blows
from Urbión to Moncayo.
High barren plains of Soria!

II

Now there will be storks in the sun,
as I look at the red evening
between Moncayo and Urbión.

III

The door opened that has
hinges in my heart,
and again the gallery
of my story appeared.

Again the small plaza
with blooming acacias,
and again the clear fountain
telling a poem of love.

IV

The brown oak
and the stone desert.
When the sun sinks behind the mountains
the river wakes up.

Oh distant mountains
of mallow and violet!
Only the river sounds
in the darkening air.

Moon turning purple
in a late evening,
in a cold field,
more moon than earth.

V

Soria of blue mountains
and violet deserts,
how many times have I dreamed of you
in this flowered plain
where the Guadalquivir
flows to the sea
between golden oranges!

VI

How many times did you blot out
these green lemon trees
with shadow from your oaks,
land of ash!

Oh fields of God,
between Urbión and Castile
and Moncayo and Aragón!

VII

In Córdoba, the mountaineer,
in Seville, the sailor
and deckhand, who has
his full sail to the sea;
where the sand sucks up
spittle from the bitter sea—
toward the Duero's fountain
my heart returned,
pure Soria . . . Oh frontier
between the earth and the moon!

High bleak country
where the young Duero flows—
land where home is!

VIII

The river wakes up.
In the dark air
only the river sounds.

Oh bitter song
of water on stone!
. . . Toward the high Hawthorn
beneath the stars.

Only the river sounds
in the valley's depths
beneath the high Hawthorn.

IX

In the middle of the field
the vacant hermitage
has its window open.

A greenish top.
Four white walls.

In the distance the stones
dazzle in the rough Guadarrama.
Shining, soundless water.

In the clear air
the thicket's small, leafless
poplars, March lyres.

En memoria de Abel Martín

In Memory of Abel Martín

While the fiery fish draws its arc
beside the cypress, beneath the richest indigo,
and the blind boy of white stone rises in the air,
and the ivory song of the green locust
throbs and vibrates in the elm,
Let us praise the Lord—
the black stamp of his kind hand—
who has commanded silence amid the clamor.

To the God of distance and absence,
of the anchor in the sea, the full sea . . .
He frees us from the world . . . He is present everywhere—
and opens paths for us to walk.

With a cup overflowing with shadow,
with this never-filled heart,
let us praise the Lord who made Nothingness
and has carved our reason out of faith.

Song to Guiomar

Your poet
thinks of you. The distance
is lemon and violet,
the countryside still green.
You come with me, Guiomar.
The day goes from oak grove
to oak grove, wearing itself out.
The train devours and devours
day and rail. The Spanish broom
turns to shadow; the gold
from the Guadarrama washes away.
Because a beautiful woman and her lover
are running away, breathless,
the full moon follows them.
The hidden rain resonates
inside a huge mountain.
Barren fields, high sky.
Across granite mountains
and others of basalt
is the sea and infinity at last.
We are going together; we are free.
Although God, as in the story
a proud king, may ride bareback
on the wind's best charger,
although he may swear to us, violently,
his vengeance,
although he may saddle thought,
free love, no one reaches it.

Today I write to you in my traveler's cell
at the hour of an imaginary rendezvous.
The heavy rain breaks the rainbow in the air,
and on the mountain its planetary sadness.
Sun and bells in the old tower.
Oh evening living and quiet
which places *nothing moves* next to *everything moves,*
childlike evening that your poet loved!
And adolescent day—
light eyes and dark muscles—
when you thought of Love, beside the fountain,
kissing your lips and holding your breasts!
Everything in this April light becomes transparent;
everything in the today of yesterday, the Yet
of which in its late hours
time sings and tells,
is based on a single melody
which is a chorus of evenings and dawns.
For you, Guiomar, this nostalgia of mine.

Meditatión del día

Day's Meditation

In front of the fiery palm
that the departing sun leaves behind,
in the silent afternoon
and in the peaceful garden,
while flowering Valencia
drinks the Guadalaviar—
Valencia of slender towers,
in the lyric sky of Ausias March,
turning its river to roses
before it reaches the sea—
I think of the war. The war
sweeps like a hurricane
across the bare plains of the high Duero,
across the tillable plains,
from fertile Extremadura
to these gardens of lemon groves,
from the gray Asturian skies
to the marshes of light and salt.
I think of Spain. Completely sold
from river to river, mountain to mountain,
sea to sea.

1937

Vicente Huidobro

Vicente Huidobro was born in Santiago de Chile in 1893 and died in 1948. In 1916 he gave a lecture during which he said that the first, second, and third conditions of the poet are to create. Thus he was branded a "creationist." He saw the poet's mission as the making of autonomous poetic images, presenting an invented world. What separates him from similar poets of the time is his subject matter. His poems are made up of images of wings, ships, trains, light, meteors, wind, angels, and birds. They are floating musical collages.

Alerta

Alert

                                                        Midnight

In the garden
Each shadow is a stream

The coming noise is not a carriage

Over the Paris sky
Otto von Zeppelin

The sirens sing
In the black waves
And this bugle which is sounding now
Is not the trumpet of Victory
                          One hundred airplanes
                          Fly around the moon

PUT OUT YOUR PIPE

Bomb shells explode like ripe roses
And the bombs pierce our days

Cut up songs
                Tremble in the branches

The wind twists the streets

HOW CAN THE STARS IN THE POND BE PUT OUT

Astro
Star

The book
        And the door
                Close in the wind

My head leans
        On the shadow of the smoke
And this blank page that is withdrawing

Listen to the noise of the living evening
        Clock of the horizon

Under the aged mist
One would say a mechanical star

        My bedroom trembles like a ship
But you are
        You alone

        The Star of my ceiling

I look at your shipwrecked memory

        And that naive bird
        Drinking the water of the mirror

Gare
Railroad Station

The troops get off
                  In the depths of night

The soldiers have forgotten their names

      Under the conic smoke
      The train departs like a telephone message

Two small wings have folded
On the shoulders of a crippled veteran

And a star has been lost in all the roads
The clouds passed by
                  Bleating toward the Orient
Someone is looking for his own footprints
Among the forgotten wings

One
    Two
        Ten
           Twenty

And that butterfly that played among the
                flowers of the pictures
Flutters around my cigar

Horizonte
Horizon

To pass the aging horizon

And to see the pulsing star
In the depths of dreams

You were so beautiful
                    that you could not talk

I went away
            But I carry in my hand
That native sky
With a worn sun

This evening
            in a café
                    I have drunk

                    A trembling liquor
                    Like a red fish

And again in the hidden glass
That filial sleep

You were so beautiful
                    that you could not talk

Something suffered in your breast

Your eyes were green
                    but I was going away

You were so beautiful
                    that I learned to sing

*Marino**

Sailor

That bird which is flying for the first time
Flies away from the nest looking backwards

with fingers to lips
              I have called you

I invented the water jets
On the tree tops

I made you the most beautiful of women
So beautiful that you blushed in the evenings

              The moon is going away from us
              And throws a wreath over the chest

I have made rivers run
              that never existed

With one cry I raised a mountain
And around it we dance a new dance

              I cut all the roses
              From the clouds of the East

And I taught a bird of snow how to sing

Let us march over the loosened months

I am the old sailor
              Who sews cut horizons

*Translator's note: This is a key poem in which Huidobro
states his poetics, which he called "Creacionismo"—
"Creationism," to distinguish it from Surrealism.*

Universo
Universe

Beneath the bower
A hardened song
                    Where are we

The world has changed places
And false stars shine in the sky

            Guitar chords on the sea

The shadow is something that flies off

            Near the voltaic arc
            Circled an airplane

                    A handerchief in the air

And no house had doors

An oblique lake
Makes space

            The road on
            the inverted field

Tomorrow will be the end of the universe

Mares Articos

Arctic Seas

The Arctic Seas
              Hanging from the sunset

A bird is burning between the clouds

Day after day
              Feathers kept falling
Over the roof tiles

Who has developed the rainbow

                           There is no rest

        My bed
              Was as soft as wings

Over the Arctic Seas

I search for the lark which flew from my breast

Enrique Lihn

Enrique Lihn (1929–88) writes with the intensity of a Biblical prophet who has just returned from the desert, with the difference that now we lack a personal God, a salvation. Reality has exposed Lihn; he seems to have lost his innocence early. But whether it is loss of political faith, religious faith or faith in erotic love, he faces it with courage and honesty and transmits his suffering directly.

Nicanor Parra calls Lihn an anti-poet. I would call him an impure poet, more interested in what he has to say than how he says it. He uses whatever strategy is necessary to get across his perceptions. He is aware that the poet has many selves—stranger, prophet, narrator, buffoon, pontiff. Because he allows his many voices to speak, he can be as lyrical as Machado, as searing as Vallejo or as ironic as Brecht.

La pieza oscura
The Dark Room

The mixture of air in the dark room, as if the bare ceiling
    threatened
a vague bloody drizzle.
Of that liquor we inhaled, the dirty nose, symbol of
    innocence and of precocity
to renew our struggle together secretly, but we did not know
    we did not ignore what cause;
a game of hands and feet, twice villainous, but equally sweet
as the first loss of blood avenged with teeth and nails or,
    for a girl
sweet as the first flow of her blood.

And so the old wheel began to revolve—symbol of life—
    the wheel that gets stuck as if it did not fly,
between one generation and the other, in the winking
    of bright and dark eyes
with an imperceptible mossy sound.
Centering on its axle, in imitation of the children who used
    to roll two by two, with red ears—symbol of modesty
    that savors its offense—angrily tender,
the wheel partly revolved as if in an old age prior
    to the invention of the wheel
clockwise and counter clockwise.

For a moment confusion reigned over time. And I bit
    into the neck of my cousin Isabel for a long time,
in a winking of the eye of one who sees everything,
    as if in an age prior to sin
because we pretended to struggle in the belief that we
    were doing so; belief on the edge of faith
    like a game on truth
and the facts scarcely dared to disbelieve us
with red ears.

We stopped revolving on the floor, my cousin Angel victor
    over Pauline, my sister; and I over Isabel, both nymphs
wrapped in a bud of blankets that made them sneeze—
    the smell of naphthalene in a fuzzing fruit.
Those were our victorious weapons and their beaten ones
    mixing up one with the other in the manner of nests
    like cells, of cells like hugs, of hugs like chains
    on the feet and on the hands.
We stopped revolving with a strange feeling of shame, without
    managing to formulate a reproach
other than having to demand such an easy success.
The wheel was revolving perfectly, as in the time of its
    apparition in the myth, as in its age of its wood
    recently worked
with a sound of medieval sparrows' song;
the time was flying in a good direction. It would be heard
    advancing toward us
much faster than the dining room clock whose ticking
    was burning to break so much silence.
Time flew as if to flood with a sound of foaming waters
    faster in the nearness of the mill's wheel,
    with sparrows' wings—symbols of the free savage
    order—with all of it as the single overflowing object
and life—symbol of the wheel—speeds up to pass
    tempestuously making the wheel revolve at an accelerated
    speed, as in a grinding of time, tempestuous.
I let my captive go and fell on my knees as if I had grown
    old suddenly, preyed on by sweet, cloying panic
as if I had known, beyond love in the flower of its age,
    the cruelty of the heart in the fruit of love,
    the corruption of the fruit and then . . . the bloody core,
    feverish and dry.

What will become of the children we were? Someone plunged to
    turn on the light, faster than the thought of grown-ups.
They were already looking for us inside the house, around
    the mill: the room dark as the clearing of a forest.
But there was always time to gain it from the eternal
    child hunters. When they came into the dining room,
    there we were sitting at the table like angels
glancing at our illustrated magazines—the men at one end,
    the women at the other—
in perfect order, according to blood.

The wheel detached itself from counter clockwise
    before revolving and neither could we ourselves meet
    at the turning of vertigo, when we entered time
as in still waters, serenely fast;
we scattered ourselves in them forever, the equal
    of the remainder of the same shipwreck.
But a part of me has not revolved to the rhythm of the wheel
    with the stream.
Nothing is real enough for a ghost. I am in part that boy
    who falls on his knees
sweetly overcome by impossible omens
and I have not completely come of age yet
nor will I obey like him
once and for all.

Caleta
Cove

In this white village of dark fishermen
love lives at two steps from hate
and tenderness, dead, takes refuge in a sleep
that magnifies the look of the village madman.

Dawn: the sea falls asleep beneath the sun
like a drunken giant after a battle;
last night someone lost his life in its hands
gloved with white more cruel than snow.
But the dead man's companions returned
to their scallop shells gorged with bloody seed
and lay their dying trophies on the sand.

Noon: the tattooed sit at the table
and their women guard their backs
wary of the dangerous gestures that order
another glass of wine
more madly each time.
Soon, the sexual war
and the working men come down to the beach
as to one more mocked mistress
to row in a furious sleep of drunkards.

Shipyard of the sun wounded by heaven
in the fire trenches of the waves.
It is time to go to the sea to snare its birds
unless a fight between men, dogs or roosters
fails to hold the boat-hound by the wateredge.

Night brings some peace to the cove:
a little fresh water, that in the madman's eyes
is stirred by the oblivion of itself.
Someone I have not been able to forget grows inside me
like the surge of a sea captive to the moon
and pounds my face from inside until it blinds me.

Gallo
Rooster

This rooster that comes from far off in his song,
lit up by the first rays of the sun;
this king that shapes himself in my window with his living
      crest, hatefully,
does not ask or answer, screams in the Banquet Hall
as if his guests the gargoyles did not exist
and he were more lonely than his screams.

He screams of stone, of antiquity, of nothing,
fights against my sleep but ignores it;
his wives mean nothing to him nor the corn that will make
      him kiss the dust in the afternoon.
He limits himself to howling like a heretic in the fire of his own feathers.
And he is a gigantic horn
that darkness blows as it falls into Hell.

Barro
Mud

I

Mud, endless malice. All source ends by yielding
to the pressure of this original matter.
The days of the water are numbered, but not so the days of the mud
that takes the place of water when the well is filled.
Not so the days of the mud that returns us to the seventh day.
As children we played with it, it is not strange that it plays with us,
those created in the image and likeness of it.

II

God the Father, God the Son, God the Holy Ghost:
earth and water; then the mud that was in the beginning.
One single feeling in the origin of everyone:
this endless malice.

III

Sooner or later we will be reasonable again.
It is in the order of things, nothing is known about them
     until we take them with relative calm,
as if nothing had happened.

IV

There is nothing more strange than one's self. It is
     the appearance of another who ended up visiting us
by finally accepting a repeated invitation.
It seemed to me that I saw my shadow when I opened the door,
     just as we were about to leave.
The show had started. "Come in. Come in."
"We were waiting for you," I said and she said, "I do not
     recognize the ungrateful,"
with a curious trembling in the voice.

La invasion
The Invasion

In the antiseptic Council Hall a plumed head was set
      on a throne
and, as if nothing had happened in a thousand years,
      a clattering silence ruled there again
that the fire was going to break with its single word
over the sacrificial stone.
The same unchangeable boys struck the ritual posture,
stripped to the waist with their feet on the table,
      chewing tobacco;
their tattoos spoke for them, those childhood treasures
were the same issue of an illustrated magazine
and they were gathered at the end of the cartoon strip
waiting for their victim's election.

The sign of crossed swords was made.
The heraldic eagle was uncaged at the service door,
      the advice being to carry out the butchery calmly
without loss of one accusing feather. Other stupid
      measures were taken.
A finger bowl was brought to the young emperor's table
      for hands that were bloody with ink.
His cut-throat letters were acknowledged,
      in a terribly obsequious tropical English.
Outside the evil was marching quietly in place. It still
      waited for some hours in the courtyard
just in case something was forgotten.
And the mercenaries sang the hymn
of a pack of dogs on the way to the island.

Market Place

      Tall wax candles that burn forever,
stone jets, towers of this city
in which, forever, I am passing
like death itself: poet and stranger;
marvelous ship of stone in which kings
and gargoyles watch over my dark existence.
The old weavers of Europe drink, sing
and dance altogether and solely for themselves.
Only night does not change places,
on board ship even the night watchmen
with their beaten faces know it. Not even stone escapes
—it is the same everywhere—the passing of night.

Ciudades
Cities

Cities are images.
All you need is a schoolboy text
to live the absurd life of poetry
in its first infancy:
strangeness raised to the cube of Dürer,
and a pain that cannot, itself, be
melancholy.

Two white rats revolve in a circle
to the speed of neurosis;
after going around and around for exactly sixty days
in the great world as in a cage,
I concentrate on only one thought:
revolving rats.

White, hairy, small sphere
split into halves that leap to be joined again,
but where the cut was, the puzzled softness
and the pain, now are little legs,
and between them dividing sexes,
compensating sexes.
Things are coming out from where we were beings
apart completely, completely apart.
Five minutes of hatred, total . . . five minutes.

Cities are the same as getting lost in the same
old street, in that part of the world, never in another.

What is it that would not mean the same
if the petty being, identical to what is different,
were returned to the whole, in two words?
Sun of the last day; what a great final period
for poetry and her work.

In the great world as in a cage
I tune a dangerous instrument.

Nathalie

We were about to do a perfect job,
Nathalie in a stone house in Provence.
Now you will say it was all bad from the beginning,
      but the truth is that we dug up,
      as if by magical art
all, incredibly all, the bones of love
and as far as I am concerned the last breath of it:
the bouquet of lavender flowers.
    It is true: our good intentions failed,
      our projects reduced to the dust
      of the road
between Lulu's house and yours.
It was not possible to go any further with the children
who besides pissed all over our experiment;
but I discovered Michaux in your house, Nathalie:
      a shouting I was missing,
a pain again, too great to be measured,
for which words taste like nothing.
    I returned to Paris with an empty notebook,
your ass in place of my head,
your marvelous legs rather than my own arms,
the heart I do not know whether in the hole of your
      stomach or mine.
We exchanged everything, eating each other: organs
      and memories, accidents for the effort made
      trying to dig too deep,
Nathalie, for blending in a single pulp.
    To believe in God; that is the last straw
and to complete, chewing it like cud, the cycle of babbling
all over France.
But yes we worked hard,
shoulder to shoulder, navel to navel
and we were about to submerge in Rilke.

We have lost nothing:
this pain is all that could be expected;
to have it at the right moment is the final straw,
      my little old woman, my wasp, my mother
      of two sons almost mine, my womb.
"Va faire dodo Alexandre. Va faire dodo Gerome."
      Ah, what a relief for them
reconciliation's flow of babble. All other
      form of cult is shit.
I become literature.
This poem is all that could be expected
after such a job, Nathalie.

Epilogue

We all live in darkness, separated
by flimsy walls full of false doors;
there will be coins withdrawn for petty expenses
      of friendship or love our conversations
against the inexhaustible are not sufficient to touch it
now that it is necessary to renew them, to take
a different road to arrive at the same.
It is necessary to get into the habit of knowing
how to live day by day, each man on his own,
as in the best of all possible worlds.
Our dreams prove it: we are split in two.
We can sympathize with each other,
and that is more than enough: that is all, and it is hard
to place our personal history next to another's,
pruning from the excess that we are
to distract the attention of what is impossible to attract it
      above the coincidences,
and not to insist, not to insist too much:
to be a good narrator who plays his part
between buffoon and pontiff.

Olzhas Suleimenov

Olzhas Suleimenov is a contemporary poet from Kazakhstan. He is also a geologist and anti-nuclear activist. Before the breakup of the Soviet Union, Suleimenov was instrumental in stopping nuclear testing in Kazakhstan. I had intended to do a chapbook of Suleimenov translations, but his recent work is hard to find.

—*Seattle, 1991*

Blind Man

I saw a blind man in the Louvre:
Solitary, silent; no guide.
His eye sockets stared
At a painting of Venus—
Just as the black laborers
Looked into "The Heart of Darkness."
One could hear the floorboards creaking,
It was so quiet.
The blind man paused before a huge
Canvas—somehow he saw it.
Through the scars on his face?
No, it was with his eyes:
Like a sighted man slowly reading a book,
He thumbed from painting to painting,
And then he stopped again;
Stood for ten minutes
Before a bare space.